CUTTING-EDGE **router tips & tricks**

CUTTING-EDGE
router
tips & tricks

How to get the most out of your router

JIM STACK

POPULAR
WOODWORKING
BOOKS

CINCINNATI, OHIO
www.popularwoodworking.com

Cutting-Edge Router Tips & Tricks. Copyright © 2005 by Jim Stack. Printed and bound in China. All rights reserved. No part of this book may be reproduced in any form or by any electronic or mechanical means, including information storage and retrieval systems, without permission in writing from the publisher, except by a reviewer, who may quote brief passages in a review. Published by Popular Woodworking Books, an imprint of F+W Publications, Inc., 4700 East Galbraith Road, Cincinnati, Ohio, 45236. First edition.

Visit our Web site at www.popularwoodworking.com for information on more resources for woodworkers.

Other fine Popular Woodworking Books are available from your local bookstore or direct from the publisher.

09   08   07   06   05   5   4   3   2   1

Library of Congress Cataloging-in-Publication Data

Stack, Jim, 1951-
    Cutting-edge router tips & tricks : how to get the most out of your
        router / Jim Stack p. cm.
    Includes index.
    ISBN 1-55870-713-1 (hardcover: alk. paper)
    ISBN 1-55870-698-4 (paperback: alk. paper)
    1. Routers (Tools) 2. Woodwork. 3. Jig and fixtures. I. Title: Router
tips & tricks. II. Title: Cutting-edge router tips and tricks. III. Title.

TT203.5.S73 2005
684'.08--dc22   2004054690

Editor: Amy Hattersley
Designer: Brian Roeth
Layout artist: Joni DeLuca
Production coordinator: Robin Richie
Photographer: Al Parrish (pages 2, 9, 92, 102, 116)
Book photographer: Jim Stack
Technical illustrator: Jim Stack

READ THIS IMPORTANT SAFETY NOTICE

To prevent accidents, keep safety in mind while you work. Use the safety guards installed on power equipment; they are for your protection. When working on power equipment, keep fingers away from saw blades, wear safety goggles to prevent injuries from flying wood chips and sawdust, wear headphones to protect your hearing and consider installing a dust vacuum to reduce the amount of airborne sawdust in your woodshop. Don't wear loose clothing, such as neckties or shirts with loose sleeves, or jewelry, such as rings, necklaces or bracelets, when working on power equipment. Tie back long hair to prevent it from getting caught in your equipment. People who are sensitive to certain chemicals should check the chemical content of any product before using it. The authors and editors who compiled this book have tried to make the contents as accurate and correct as possible. Plans, illustrations, photographs and text have been carefully checked. All instructions, plans and projects should be carefully read, studied and understood before beginning construction. Due to the variability of local conditions, construction materials, skill levels, etc., neither the author nor Popular Woodworking Books assumes any responsibility for any accidents, injuries, damages or other losses incurred as a result of the material presented in this book. Prices listed for supplies and equipment were current at the time of publication and are subject to change. Glass shelving should have all edges polished and must be tempered. Untempered glass shelves may shatter and can cause serious bodily injury. Tempered shelves are very strong and if they break will just crumble, minimizing personal injury.

METRIC CONVERSION CHART

to convert	to	multiply by
Inches	Centimeters	2.54
Centimeters	Inches	0.4
Feet	Centimeters	30.5
Centimeters	Feet	0.03
Yards	Meters	0.9
Meters	Yards	1.1
Sq. Inches	Sq. Centimeters	6.45
Sq. Centimeters	Sq. Inches	0.16
Sq. Feet	Sq. Meters	0.09
Sq. Meters	Sq. Feet	10.8
Sq. Yards	Sq. Meters	0.8
Sq. Meters	Sq. Yards	1.2
Pounds	Kilograms	0.45
Kilograms	Pounds	2.2
Ounces	Grams	28.4
Grams	Ounces	0.035

For all the woodworkers who own
or will soon own a router

About the Author

Jim Stack is the Acquisitions Editor for Popular Woodworking Books. Before that he worked in commercial cabinet- and furniture-making shops for 20 years.

Acknowledgements

Thanks to my Popular Woodworking Books team, namely, associate editor Amy Hattersley, designer Brian Roeth and production coordinator Robin Richie for their help and patience in creating yet another great-looking book!

Thanks to Al Parrish for his photos of the finished projects. He's an artist with light.

I would like to acknowledge the countless woodworkers that have taught me (knowingly and unknowingly) about design, techniques and how to use tools. I learn something new every day by watching you do what you do best.

When I saw the jig that John Hutchinson made for routing the lids on his shell boxes, I knew it was a perfect addition to this book. Thanks for your infectious creativity John!

table of contents

introduction

Routers are noisy, make lots of dust and can be dangerous. Did I say they're loud, dirty and can jump out of your hands? So why do woodworkers have a love affair with this handheld power tool?

The router has been around for 70 or 80 years now, and hasn't changed in looks much at all. A router is a motor mounted inside a housing. The motor's shaft has a collet on one end to which steel cutters can be mounted. The first routers were large (you definitely needed two hands to operate them), had steel housings (which made them heavy) and motors that could give you a good jolt if they wanted to. Router motors are now double-insulated and the housings are made of high-impact plastic, both of which mean you won't get shocked if something shorts out unexpectedly. Also, they are smaller and lighter in weight, so sometimes you only need one hand to operate the router.

By definition, to rout means to cut or plow a groove or furrow. A router is the tool that does just that. However, it was discovered early on that the router could be fitted with cutters and guided along the edges of boards to cut moulding profiles. Not only that, it could cut grooves and tenons and make joints!

Hundreds (dare I say thousands) of cutters and bits are available for use in the router. This tool has added a whole arsenal for woodworkers to use in building cabinets and furniture. Those of us who have worked in commercial cabinet- and furniture-making shops have used the router for just about everything, from cutting grooves and profiles to edge-joining boards and cutting panels to size. Home woodworkers are now able to perform all these operations.

Frame and panel construction, splined joints, dadoes, rabbets, mortise-and-tenon joinery, casings and mouldings of every possible variety, jointing and planing are a few of the operations that can be done with the router. The router can also hollow out containers, cut circles and ellipses, trim veneers and plastic laminates, cut thin sheets of aluminum, and the list goes on.

Using the router requires taking some precautions to protect yourself. Earmuffs or plugs to protect your hearing, and a dust mask to protect your lungs. Double-checking your setups whenever you use the router will protect your hands, body and peace of mind.

I won't tell you to fear the router, because that's unhealthy and can make you paranoid, but I will tell you to respect the router and what it can do and learn what it's capable of doing. Having said that, enjoy using this awesome tool!

One thing to remember about using the router (or any power tool for that matter) is that you're smarter than the tool. But it needs to be respected for its power and quickness. You can't think as fast as the tool can operate, so think ahead when making setups.

routers

ROUTERS ARE AVAILABLE IN THREE styles: trimmer, fixed-base and plunge. Each type has talents and abilities the others don't. This chapter will give you an overview of each style and help you decide which one is best for your particular needs.

As stated earlier, the general look and operation of the router hasn't changed since it was invented, but lots of extras have been added that have given the router a new lease on life: interchangeable bases, tons of new cutters and better motors.

A router can last 20 to 30 years or more if properly maintained. It has few moving parts, and those that do move can be easily repaired or replaced. Now, on to the good stuff.

■ *styles of routers*

The trimmer router is the smallest of the routers and the least powerful, but that's what makes it unique. It can be held and operated with one hand and easily guided when routing signs or patterns.

The main use of the trimmer is just that — for trimming high-pressure laminates, thin sheets of nonferrous metals and wood veneers. After high-pressure laminate has been put onto a substrate, it needs to be trimmed flush to the edges of the substrate. A straight- or bevel-cutting bit with a guide bearing is used to do the trimming. The thickness of the laminate or veneer is usually $\frac{1}{8}$" or less, so not a lot of power is needed for these cutting operations.

I had occasion to install a sign on a storefront in a mall. The sign's letters were made of wood that I attached to the storefront about 15 feet off the ground. Then the letters had to be laminated with thin sheets of polished brass. The brass needed to be trimmed after it had been applied, and that's when the trimmer router paid for itself. I was balancing on a ladder and holding the router above my head, trimming off the extra metal. The router was light enough that I could have a hand free to steady myself and still get the job done before the mall opened for the day.

Trimmer routers are great for making signage and cutting grooves for inlays. If fitted with a fence on the base and a $\frac{1}{8}$"-diameter straight-cutting bit, the trimmer can rout a $\frac{1}{16}$"-deep groove around the edges of Federal-style table legs or the edges of the top. Strips of wood veneer in-

The trimmer router is small and can be controlled easily with one hand. It's great for cutting thin metal and high-pressure laminates and cutting mortises for small hinges.

lays can be set into these perfectly cut grooves.

Another good use of the trimmer router is cutting mortises for butt hinges. The base of the router is small enough to fit into a template so guide bushings aren't needed. The base of the router can ride right on the work and remain stable.

The base of a trimmer router can be fitted with guide bushings that will follow templates, or they can be used freehand to create designs. Woodcarvers use them to remove large amounts of material so they can then use their chisels to do the fine work.

A fixed-base router has a base that can be moved up and down the body of the router, but only when the router is not running. Fixed-base routers range from $\frac{1}{2}$ horsepower (hp) up to $3\frac{1}{2}$ hp. The bases

will accept guide bushings and usually come with a custom-fitted adjustable fence.

A plunge router can be moved up and down inside the base by releasing a finger-operated lever. This can be done while the router is running, which makes it easy to cut mortises, for example. The router is put into position over the workpiece and can then be pushed or plunged into the work. Plunge routers are $1\frac{1}{2}$ hp up to $3\frac{1}{2}$ hp.

A combination of a fixed-base and plunger router is available. A single router motor can have either base installed on it in seconds.

The fixed-base router is the standard for routers. The base can be adjusted for cutting depth, and a variety of attachments and jigs can be attached to the base.

■ *router bits*

In the last 10 years, bit and cutter manufacturers have gone all out to serve router users — commercial and home woodworkers. We now have an almost unlimited choice of size, shape, profile and style of router bits. These include bits that cut square grooves, round-bottomed grooves, V-shaped grooves, edge roundovers, coves, ogees, bevels, cope-and-stick joints, raised panels, finger joints, scarf joints, dovetails, combinations of coves and roundovers, small crown moulding, base trim, chair rail, door and window casing, mullions, rabbets, undercut picture-hanging grooves, T-shaped slots, full-bullnose profiles, and the list goes on. Every time I go to my local woodworking supplies store, I see a new style of router bit.

Most router bits come with guide bearings, which means the bit can be guided along the edge of a workpiece or can follow a template. These bearings are located on the ends or up on the shafts of the bits. The bits with the bearings mounted on

their shafts can be used with plunge routers and guided by a template to cut virtually any shape you desire. I use them when I cut the kidney-shaped cavities on the backs of the solid-body guitars that I build.

All router bits are available with carbide steel cutters. Carbide steel has proven itself to stay sharper and cooler under high-speed usage than any other type of cutter steel, which makes it perfect for router bits. For the home woodworker, this means a router bit can be used for years without needing sharpening. Even commercial woodworkers can get miles and miles out of one sharpening.

Router bits are made with $\frac{1}{4}$"- and $\frac{1}{2}$"-diameter shanks. Whenever possible, buy the $\frac{1}{2}$"-diameter shanked bits. They are much stronger and will run a little cooler. During the writing of this book, I broke a $\frac{1}{4}$"-diameter router bit. They just can't take the pressure!

This is a good starter set of router bits. Left to right, straight-cutting with guide bearing on the shank, straight-cutting, dovetail, straight-cutting with guide bearing, cove cutter, roundover and bevel. Get the best router bits you can afford. Just like most things, if it seems like a "good deal," it probably isn't in the long run. It could have inferior carbide steel in the cutters, possibly weaker steel in the shanks, and shoddy guide bearings. This can be dangerous if one or all of these components fail under usage.

■ **SAFETY FIRST**

Changing Router Bits

- Always unplug the router before you change router bits.
- Before plugging the router in, make sure the switch is in the *off* position.

■ *changing router bits*

Changing router bits is easy. Using two wrenches in one hand, it's a quick matter of squeezing the wrenches together. This photo shows the configuration of the wrenches for tightening the collet nut. When you feel the nut snug up, squeeze a little more and you're done. Don't over-tighten the nut. If the collet won't hold the bit after you've tightened the nut, replace the collet.

To loosen the collet nut, reverse the wrenches as shown in this photo.

replacing motor brushes

Unless a router is dropped on the floor or falls in a lake, not much is likely to go wrong with it. Routers have motors that require brushes to rub against their armatures so they can get electric power to turn the motor. Inspect the brushes often to see how they look. To remove and re-place the brushes (there are two, one opposite the other), remove the plastic cap that holds the brush in place.

This brush, the gray thing with the wire and spring attached to it, is in good shape. If it's less than $1/4$" long, it should be replaced. You can order these brushes from any tool repair shop. Simply put the new brush in the slot and reinstall the plastic cap.

Corded Power Tools

When you're finished using a corded power tool, set it on a surface out of your walking area and coil up the cord. Many times I've seen power tools go crashing to the floor when someone's foot caught on the power cord hanging off the worktable. This can ruin a tool beyond repair if it lands just the wrong way — and they always do.

[REPLACING MOTOR BRUSHES CONTINUED]

Routers are awesome power tools, but they are noisy and create tons of dust. Protect your hearing with earmuffs or earplugs. Earmuffs are good when you're in a situation where you don't need constant hearing protection. They're quick to put on and take off. Earplugs offer great protection and can be worn all day long if you're working with or around tools that run constantly. The dust mask shown here is one of the best I've ever used. It has filters that can be easily replaced. A valve lets you breathe in through the filters only. When you exhale, the valve reverses to let that air out unfiltered. Don't bother with dust masks like doctors wear. They don't seal around your face, and they aren't made to filter out fine dust particles. If your lungs and ears are important to you, use the proper protective gear.

Feeding Stock Past a Router Bit

Never, ever, feed stock *between* a router bit and a fence. If the fence is mounted on a router table or a router base, it doesn't matter. The router isn't like the table saw. On a table saw, it's essential for the work to be cut to width between the blade and fence. The rotation of a router bit is horizontal to the cut being made and this rotation will pull the workpiece into the router bit. This will throw the work across the shop and pull your fingers into the cutter. This is not to be taken lightly. I've seen otherwise tough guys turn white when this has happened to them. I had one boss that would fire any employee on the spot if they violated this rule. It can endanger you and anyone else that might be in the shop.

Here's yet another use for duct tape. A plastic attachment for a standard vacuum cleaner can be taped to the base of your router. When you use the router, simply plug the business end of your shop vacuum to this attachment. You might need to use a reducing attachment on the hose of the shop vacuum to plug into the attachment on the router base.

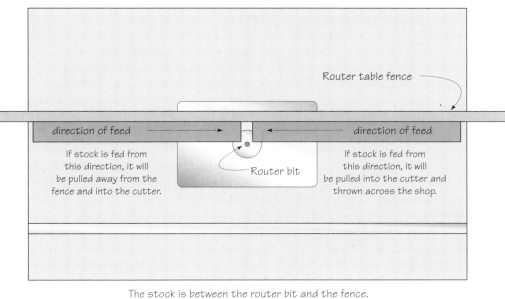

Router table fence

direction of feed →   ← direction of feed

If stock is fed from this direction, it will be pulled away from the fence and into the cutter.

Router bit

If stock is fed from this direction, it will be pulled into the cutter and thrown across the shop.

The stock is between the router bit and the fence.
This is a very dangerous setup and is not to be done under any circumstances!

router table

THIS ROUTER TABLE DESIGN IS A composite of ideas I've seen over the years. This is not the ultimate router table; there is no such thing. I have taken the best tricks that I thought would make a router table that is easy to use. I'm not ashamed to admit I "borrow" all the good ideas I can for my woodworking projects. We can all learn from each other. It's my hope that someone will add another cool trick or two to this router table.

I will admit the router carriage and lift are somewhat complicated and require some precision to make. But never fear! If you follow the construction steps and use the cutting lists and illustrations to help you visualize the final project, you'll be able to make this table with no worries. The materials to make the table are inexpensive and readily available at any home-improvement center or lumberyard. The whole project (minus the router!) costs about $60. The top and insert are available from a manufacturer (see the suppliers at the back of the book), but I've included the materials you'd need to make your own.

I highly recommend that you use a router with at least 3 hp or more with this, or any, router table. For years I used a 1½ hp router and it worked, but it had to work too hard and sometimes the results weren't the best. The added horsepower does make a difference. It makes it easier to use large cutters, and the final cuts are much smoother and cleaner than a smaller horsepower router would give.

When using a router table and a large horsepower router, you need to be aware of some safety concerns.

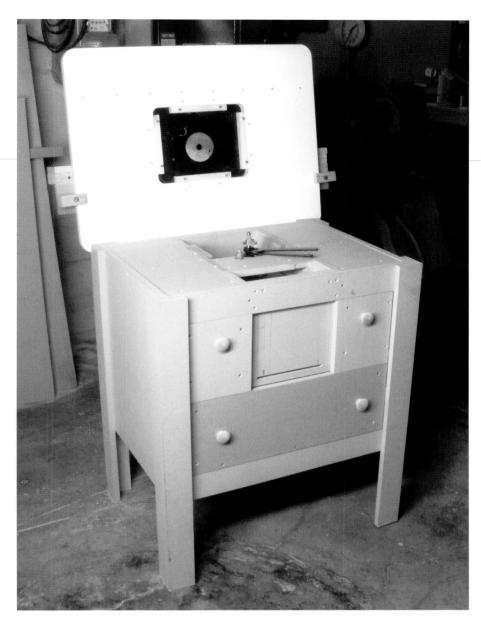

What we've done is turn our router into a stationary power tool called a shaper. Any commercial woodworker who has used or been around a shaper will tell you it can be the most dangerous power tool in the shop. Shapers and routers spin at incredibly high speeds. The average speeds on routers vary from 10,000 to 20,000 rotations per minute. That's more than 150 to well over 300 rotations per second. The speed at which things can be thrown from the cutters is over 100 miles per hour. None of us can think that fast.

That's why we use featherboards, push boards and shrouds around the cutters to protect our fingers, hands, eyes and other body parts. Whenever I make a setup on the router table, I run through my mental checklist. Is the collet nut tight and the router bit secure? Is the fence set correctly and tightened down? Are any other attachments securely in place? Then I run through it one more time. This routine has saved me some potential injuries on several occasions. Check twice before powering up.

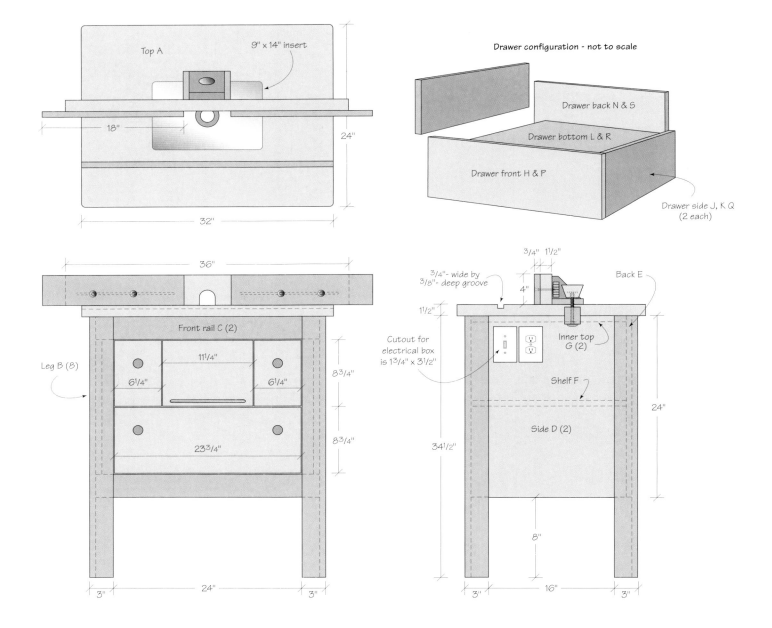

Top A

9" x 14" insert

18"

24"

32"

Drawer configuration - not to scale

Drawer back N & S

Drawer bottom L & R

Drawer front H & P

Drawer side J, K Q
(2 each)

36"

Front rail C (2)

11¹/₄"

Leg B (8)

6¹/₄"

6¹/₄"

8³/₄"

8³/₄"

23³/₄"

24"

3"

3"

3/4" 1¹/₂"

3/4"- wide by
3/8"- deep groove

Back E

4"

1¹/₂"

Cutout for
electrical box
is 1³/₄" x 3¹/₂"

Inner top
G (2)

Shelf F

Side D (2)

24"

34¹/₂"

8"

3"

16"

3"

REFERENCE	QUANTITY	PART	STOCK	THICKNESS	(mm)	WIDTH	(mm)	LENGTH	(mm)	COMMENTS
A	1	top	MDF	1½	(38)	24	(610)	36	(914)	
B	8	legs	MDF	¾	(19)	3	(76)	30	(762)	45° miter one long edge, glue 2 parts to make 1 leg
C	2	front rails	MDF	¾	(19)	3	(76)	28½	(724)	
D	2	sides	MDF	¾	(19)	3	(76)	20½	(521)	
E	1	back	MDF	¾	(19)	24	(610)	28½	(724)	
F	1	shelf	MDF	¾	(19)	19¾	(502)	28½	(724)	
G	2	inner tops	MDF	¾	(19)	19¾	(502)	28½	(724)	
H	2	drawer fronts	MDF	¾	(19)	6¼	(159)	8¾	(222)	
J	2	drawer sides	MDF	¾	(19)	8	(203)	16	(406)	
K	2	drawer sides	MDF	¾	(19)	8	(203)	19	(483)	
L	1	drawer bottom	MDF	¾	(19)	4¾	(121)	16	(406)	
M	1	drawer bottom	MDF	¾	(19)	4¾	(121)	19	(483)	
N	2	drawer backs	MDF	¾	(19)	6¼	(159)	8	(203)	
P	1	drawer front	MDF	¾	(19)	8¾	(222)	23¾	(603)	
Q	2	drawer sides	MDF	¾	(19)	8½	(216)	13	(330)	
R	1	drawer bottom	MDF	¾	(19)	23	(584)	13	(330)	
S	1	drawer back	MDF	¾	(19)	6¼	(159)	18	(457)	
T	4	drawer guides	MDF	¾	(19)	1⁹⁄₁₆	(40)	19¾	(502)	

HARDWARE

1	set 18" (457mm) drawer slides
4	1¼" (32mm) wooden knobs
2	3" (76mm) butt hinges
2	duplex electrical boxes
1	duplex outlet fixture
1	on/off switch
1	9" (229mm) x 14" (356mm) piece of ⅜" (10mm) acrylic plastic or plywood

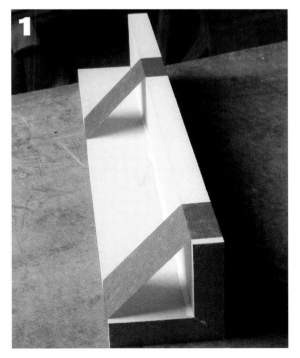

Cut out the legs, front rails, sides, back and bottom as shown in the cutting list. Tape, glue and fold the miter joints on the legs.

Using screws and glue, attach the sides to the legs. Make two of these assemblies.

Using glue and screws, attach the back to the side assemblies. Then drill pocket holes in the bottom and attach it to the table assembly.

Flip the assembly over and attach the front rails.

Mark the locations of the electrical boxes. Drill starter holes where the flanges of the boxes are located.

Make the cutouts using a jigsaw.

Drop the boxes into the holes and attach them to the table with screws through the mounting brackets.

Wire the switch and receptacle. If you are unsure about doing this procedure, contact a licensed electrician for advice or have him or her do it for you.

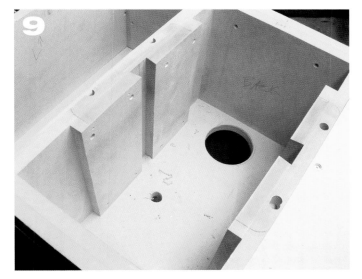

Drill a clearance hole in the bottom for the threaded rod. Also, cut a dust-collection hole in the bottom to the size needed for your dust collection system or shop vacuum.

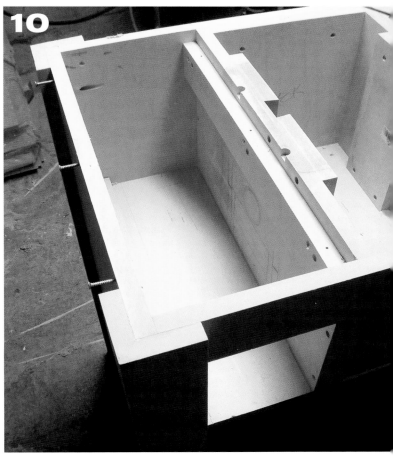

Using screws, install the upper drawer guides.

(CONTINUED ON PAGE 28)

router table carriage

REFERENCE	QUANTITY	PART	STOCK	THICKNESS	(mm)	WIDTH	(mm)	LENGTH	(mm)	COMMENTS
A	2	dovetail keepers	MDF	3/4	(19)	5	(127)	10	(254)	10° bevel one long edge
B	2	dovetail keepers	MDF	3/4	(19)	5	(127)	9 1/4	(235)	10° bevel one long edge
C	2	dovetailed guides	MDF	3/4	(19)	1 1/2	(38)	7	(178)	10° bevel two long edges
D	2	inner sides	MDF	3/4	(19)	7	(178)	11	(279)	
E	2	braces	MDF	3/4	(19)	3 1/2	(89)	7	(178)	
F	1	carriage deck plate	MDF	3/4	(19)	7	(178)	11	(279)	
G	3	collars	MDF	3/4	(19)	6 1/4	(159)	7 1/4	(184)	
H	2	front/back panels	MDF	3/4	(19)	11 1/2	(292)	11 3/4 H	(298)	
J	2	partitions	MDF	3/4	(19)	11 3/4 H	(298)	19 3/4	(502)	

HARDWARE

1	3/8"- 16 x 12" (10mm x 300mm) threaded rod
4	3/8"- 16 (10mm) hex nuts
4	3/8"- 16 (10mm) flat washers
3	3/8"- 16 (10mm) lock washers
2	3/8"- 16 (10mm) T-nuts
1	3/8"- 16 x 4" (10mm x 100mm) hex-head bolt

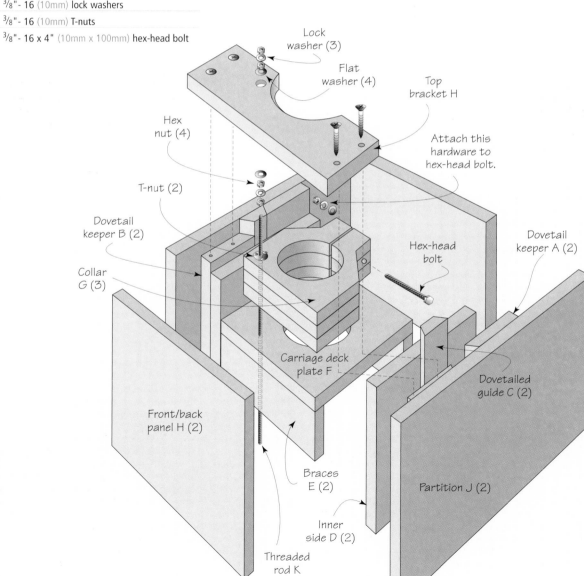

Lock washer (3)

Flat washer (4)

Top bracket H

Attach this hardware to hex-head bolt.

Hex nut (4)

T-nut (2)

Dovetail keeper B (2)

Dovetail keeper A (2)

Collar G (3)

Hex-head bolt

Carriage deck plate F

Dovetailed guide C (2)

Front/back panel H (2)

Braces E (2)

Partition J (2)

Inner side D (2)

Threaded rod K

Cut the collar parts as shown in the cutting list. Using a circle cutter in a drill press, remove the material from the centers of the parts. Make test cuts in scraps until you have a snug fit around the body of the router.

Drill clearance holes for the thread nubs that stick out on the body of the router. Locate them every 90° around the cutout.

Using the router as an alignment guide, glue the three collars into a sandwich.

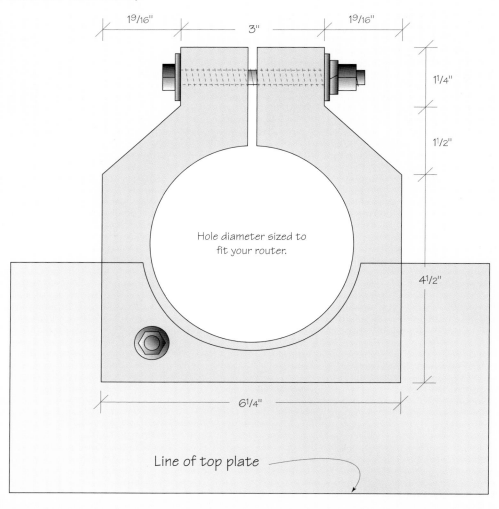

19/16"   3"   19/16"

1 1/4"

1 1/2"

Hole diameter sized to
fit your router.

4 1/2"

6 1/4"

Line of top plate

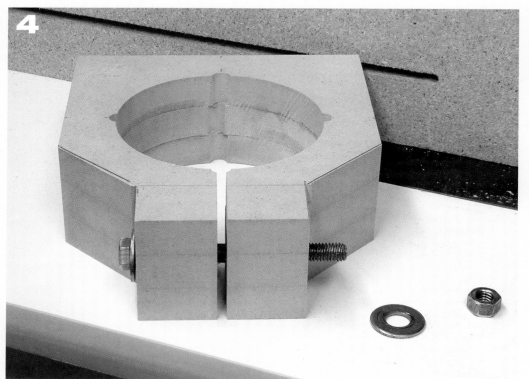

4

After the glue has dried, remove the
router from the collar assembly. Cut
the 3/16"-wide relief slot using a table
saw. Then cut the holder to shape as
shown in the illustration and drill a 3/8"-
diameter hole in the collar for the bolt.

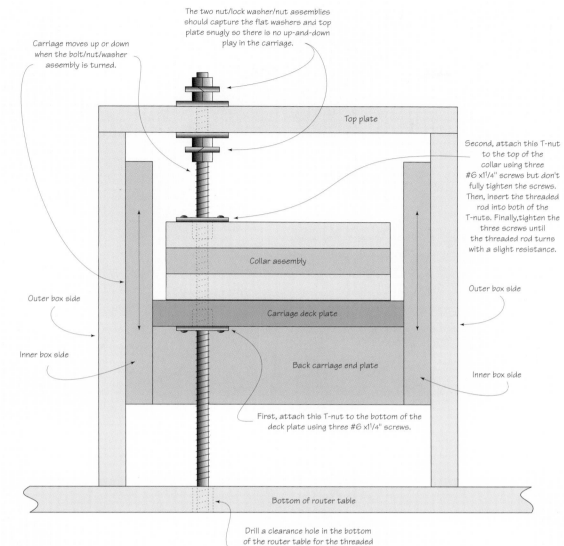

The two nut/lock washer/nut assemblies should capture the flat washers and top plate snugly so there is no up-and-down play in the carriage.

Carriage moves up or down when the bolt/nut/washer assembly is turned.

Top plate

Second, attach this T-nut to the top of the collar using three #6 x1¹/4" screws but don't fully tighten the screws. Then, insert the threaded rod into both of the T-nuts. Finally, tighten the three screws until the threaded rod turns with a slight resistance.

Collar assembly

Outer box side

Outer box side

Carriage deck plate

Inner box side

Back carriage end plate

Inner box side

First, attach this T-nut to the bottom of the deck plate using three #6 x1¹/4" screws.

Bottom of router table

Drill a clearance hole in the bottom of the router table for the threaded rod to pass through.

5

Cut out the rest of the parts for the carriage as shown in the cutting list. Build the inner carriage and outer carriage boxes. Using screws, attach one of the dovetail keepers to the inside of the outer box at the location shown in the illustration. Use one of the dovetailed guides as a spacer and attach the second dovetail keeper. Repeat this process for the opposite inside of the outer box. Using screws, attach the dovetailed guides to opposite sides of the inner box. Check the fit of the guides between the dovetail keepers. The inner box should slide with some resistance on the inside of the outer box. You don't want this inner box to freely slide up and down. Make adjustments if necessary. Attach the collar assembly to the inner box. Install the threaded rod, including the T-nuts, nuts and washers. See the illustration for details.

(CONTINUED FROM PAGE 23)

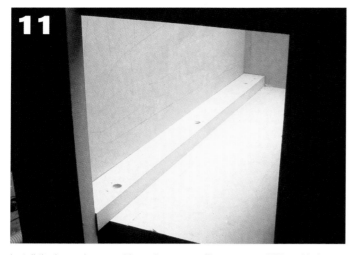

Install the lower drawer guides using screws. The purpose of this guide is to fill in the space from the side of the router table to the inside edge of the front leg. Make it $\frac{1}{16}$" wider than the space it's filling so the drawer side will have clearance past the edge of the front leg.

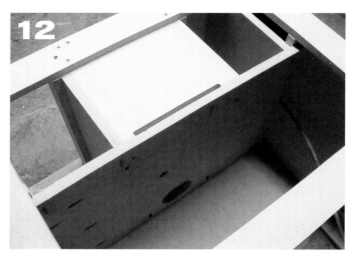

After running a few tests, I discovered that cutting a slot in the front of the carriage box helped the cross ventilation for the dust collection.

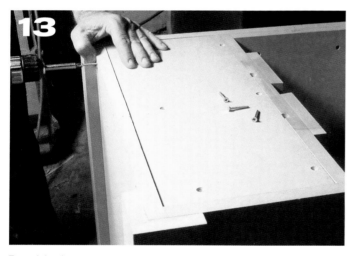

To seal the drawer compartments from unwanted dust, install the inner tops with screws. Note the line of screws in line with my fingers. These screws hold the upper drawer guide in place. This same configuration is used on the right side of the table.

Attach the other side of the dust panel with screws inserted into the right-hand upper drawer guide.

Cut out the drawer parts and assemble the drawers using screws. Drill the drawer shelf to hold router bits.

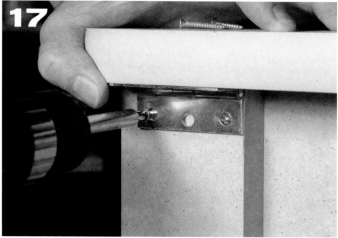

Install the drawer front with screws. These fronts also serve as drawer stops. The screw holes can be filled later if you paint the table.

Attach the top to the router table's back legs with hinges.

I laminated two pieces of particle board to make a thick fence. You could also use MDF or plywood. Laminating makes a strong, rigid fence that won't bend or cup. Glue the fence cleat to the back of the fence. Double-check for squareness.

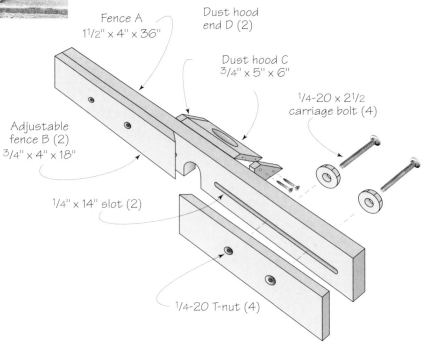

Fence A
1¹/2" x 4" x 36"

Dust hood end D (2)

Dust hood C
3/4" x 5" x 6"

1/4-20 x 2¹/2 carriage bolt (4)

Adjustable fence B (2)
3/4" x 4" x 18"

1/4" x 14" slot (2)

1/4-20 T-nut (4)

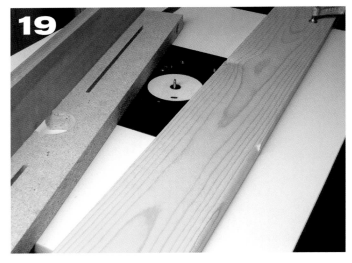

19

20

This is the first job for your new router table! Rout the stopped grooves in the fence. Create these grooves by making several shallow cuts. Don't try to cut through the fence in a single pass. Chances are good you'll break the router bit. Set up a temporary fence using a straight board and a couple of clamps.

This is the clamping setup for holding the fence to the table. This is a simple but effective way to hold the fence in place. When the top knob is tightened, the fence can't be moved.

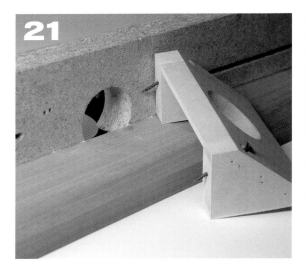

21

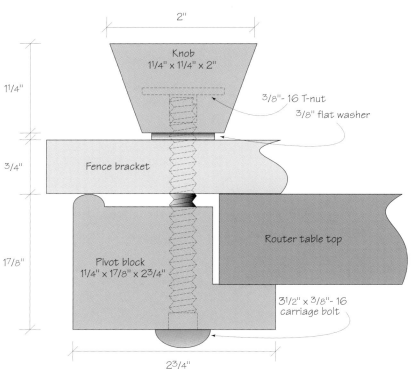

22

Attach the dust hood with a couple of 2" drywall screws.

The dust hood for the fence is made from three pieces of MDF. Cut a hole in the hood to fit your dust collector or shop vacuum hose.

2"

Knob
1¹/4" x 1¹/4" x 2"

1¹/4"

3/8"- 16 T-nut

3/8" flat washer

3/4"

Fence bracket

Pivot block
1¹/4" x 17/8" x 2³/4"

Router table top

17/8"

3¹/2" x 3/8"- 16
carriage bolt

2³/4"

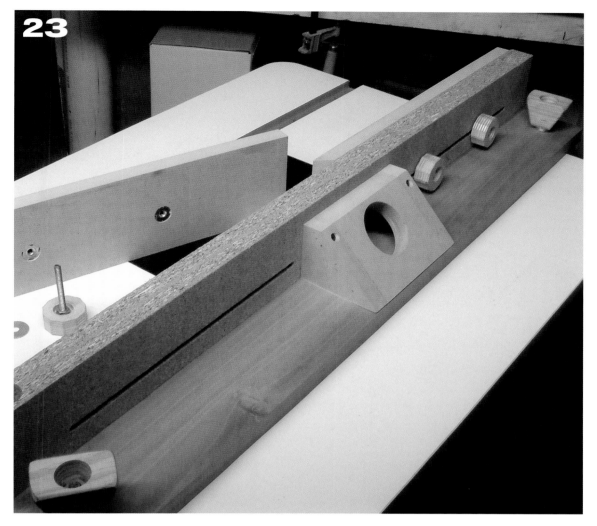

23

This photo shows the fence, the fence hold-downs, dust hood, adjustable fences and the adjustable fence knobs.

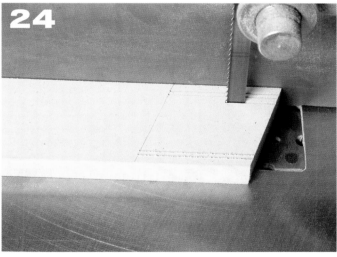

24

Make a few feather boards using a band saw. Cut a 10° - 15° angle on the end of the board and also draw that angle three or four inches from the end of the board. Set the saw's fence and make a stopped cut to this line. Flip the board and make another cut. Readjust the fence and make more cuts. Repeat until you reach the center of the board.

25

Feather boards are handy to have and are the disposable fingers you don't have to worry about hurting.

mouldings

YOU CAN MAKE CUSTOM MOULDINGS
and trim for your house or furniture and cabinet projects with a router and the proper bits.
I won't try to show you all the bits that are
available and all the possible combinations of
cuts. What I've done here is use one ogee cutter in several different ways. This will help you
see the versatility of the router.

When making moulding and trim, it's
easier to use a router mounted in a router
table. You simply feed the work through the
cutter.

If you don't have a router table, you can
make the adjustable router jig and clamp it to
a bench or sawhorse. You can also clamp the
workpiece to a bench and guide the router on
the workpiece.

Most profiling router bits have guide bearings. When using the router table, it's not necessary to use the router's guide bearing, because the fence can be adjusted to act as the guide for the workpiece. I usually leave the bearing on the bit and set the fence flush with the bearing. Hold the workpiece against the fence and move the fence until the workpiece gently touches the bearing and you're all set.

The router bit has been raised just enough to cut a small cove. A cove can make an edge look narrower and creates a nice shadow line on the moulding.

The router bit has been raised to make the full ogee profile. This setup leaves a smooth transition from the face of the moulding into the curve of the ogee.

Raising the router bit even higher will give an ogee profile with a shoulder. This adds a lot of texture to the moulding and creates several shadow lines for visual interest.

5

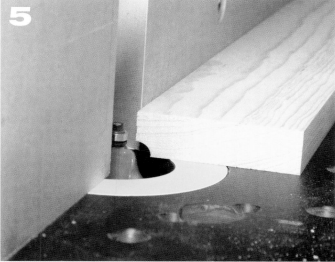

If the stock is laid face down on the router table, still more mouldings can be created using the same ogee-profile router bit. Using just the top of the router bit will cut a cove.

6

Raising the bit a little will give the full-ogee profile on your moulding.

To set off the ogee profile, raise the cutter to create a step from the face of the moulding to the start of the ogee curve.

7

8

If the router bit is raised about halfway up and the router table's fence is set away from the guide bearing, a roundover is created. The profiles and mouldings created on these two pages were made from one router bit. There are router bits available that are made with several different profiles cut into one bit. These bits are a good investment if you want to create different standard profiles and/or create your own profiles without spending a lot of money on several different speciality cutters.

cope-and-stick cutters

Several styles of matched cope-and-stick router bits are available. No matter what style you choose, the method for using them is the same. A combination cutter is available that's used to make both the long cuts and the matching end cuts on the rails. I'll show you how to use the matched cutters.

This classic cope-and-stick frame and raised-panel construction is easy to do using a router table and specially designed cutters. If you use a lot of cope-and-stick joinery, these cutters are a good investment. They will pay for themselves quickly.

1

The stock needs to be at least ¾" to 1" thick. You want enough material left on the back of the frame to hold the panel in place. You also want enough material so the profile on the front of the frame is deep enough to make it crisp and have good shadow lines. Set the router table fence so the router's guide bearings are flush with it. Make cuts on one long edge of all stiles and rails. If you're making frames with curved rails, use the router bit's guide bearing without the router fence.

2

Install the matching cutter to make the frame rail's end cuts. Lay one of the slotted cut pieces next to this cutter, using the inside edge of the groove as your guide. Align the bottom edge of the square cutter on the router bit with the top inside edge of the groove in the workpiece. This will give you a close setup for this cutter. Make a few test cuts until the rail's face is flush with the stile's face.

Use a backup board to guide the rails when making these cuts. You can cut this rail-end profile in the front edge of the backup board. The long edge of the rails will fit into this profile when making these end cuts and prevent tearing of the wood.

This panel-raising bit has a large diameter — over 3". I had to make a custom insert plate with a larger clearance hole. If you use large bits like this, you need the largest router you can get. A soft-start, variable-speed $3\frac{1}{2}$ hp router is what you should use. For a large bit, run the router motor at the slowest speed for a smoother and vibration-free cut. Not to mention it's less scary. A smaller router will spin the bit but will lose power quickly when you start feeding the panel stock into the cutter. This will strain the motor, cause premature brush wear and put undo stress on the bearings in the router. Also, the bit will heat up and burn the wood.

The panel-cutting router bit makes short work of perfectly offsetting the panel and creating a flat tenon that fits into the groove in the frame members. As always, make test cuts before you cut into your good panel stock.

The fully assembled cope-and-stick joint with a panel makes a nice door, drawer front, side or back panel for cabinets and furniture.

One more view of this joinery with the panel installed. Several different styles of panel-raising bits are available to create the look and style that fits your own personal taste.

■ *mortise-and-tenon joinery*

Mortise-and-tenon joinery is similar to cope-and-stick joinery in that they're both used to make frame and frame-and-panel doors, drawer fronts, cabinet sides and backs. The difference is that most of the time, the mortise-and-tenon frames don't have moulded edges. The edges are square and many times the panels are flat. This is typically used in Shaker furniture. This joinery is exceptionally strong and has proven itself durable for decades of use in doors and cabinet casework construction.

This is square frame-and-panel construction using mortise-and-tenon joinery. It has a simpler look than the cope-and-stick moulded frame parts. Using the router table, this joint can be made with one cutter.

The frame stock should be at least ¾" to 1"-thick. This groove cutter is designed to make a ½"-deep cut. Set the router table fence flush with the guide bearing so the full ½"-deep cut can be made. If you have curved rails, you can easily cut grooves in them without the aid of the fence. The guide bearing will ride along the curved edge of the rail.

Center the groove in the edge of the frame stock. As always, make test cuts in scrap wood until the cut is perfect.

3 Cut grooves on one long edge of all the frame parts. Then, lower the cutter until the top of the cutter is even with the bottom edge of the groove. Just use your eye for this alignment. Make a couple of test cuts and you're good to go.

4 Because the groove is centered in the edge of the frame stock, cutting the tenons is easy. Make the first cut in the rail's end, flip the rail over and make the second cut. The tenon has been completed.

5

Cuts made with sharp router bits are clean and neat. The tenon should fit snugly into the groove (or mortise) using a little hand pressure.

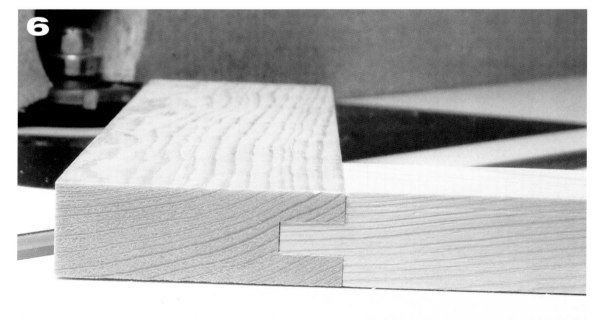

6

When this joint is assembled with glue, it will last for years to come. If you want to pin the joint through the face into the tenon for a little added strength and decoration, go ahead, but it's not necessary.

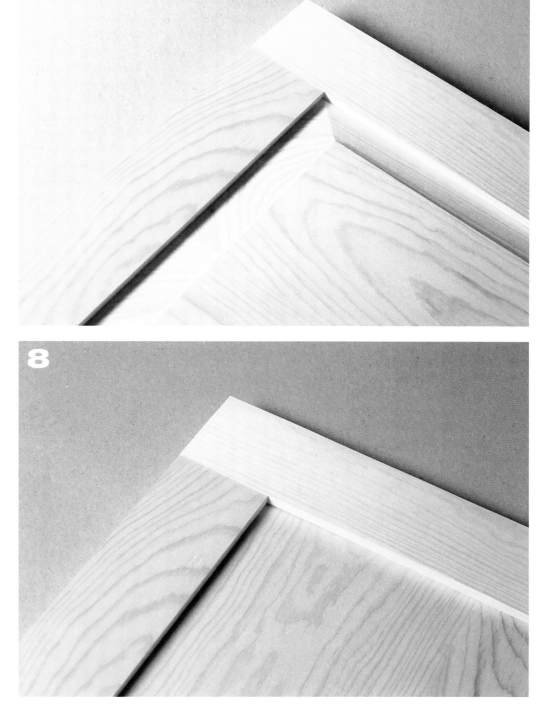

A raised panel can be used with this frame joinery. The offset of the panel adds some visual interest and extra shadow lines. A panel that is "raised" using a square rabbet cut is also an interesting choice.

8

For the cleanest and simplest look for frame-and-panel construction, this is it. Square-cut frame members are assembled using mortise-and-tenon joinery and a flat panel inside the frame. This makes a great door for cabinets and furniture. If done on a larger scale, it works well for pass-through doors in rooms of a house.

jigs, fixtures & accessories

OF ALL THE TOOLS A WOODWORKER will ever use, the router has the most uses. With the addition of shop-made add-ons that we call jigs and fixtures, the router shifts into different forms. In a router table, it becomes a shaper, planer and moulding machine. With one type of jig attached, it becomes a saw; with another, it becomes a planer.

This chapter is packed with ideas for attachments, tricks and techniques using the router. This is by no means a comprehensive list of ideas. I've included some time-tested ideas and hopefully a couple of newer ones.

Keeping safety foremost in mind, you're limited only by your imagination as to how the router can be used to perform a particular operation.

circle and arc routing jig

Using the proper jig, routing circles is easy. This jig will hold your router securely and allow you to rout circles and arcs. The adjustable block will set the center of the radius to exactly what you want. You can make round tabletops and discs for forming cylinders and arcs.

The jig can be made from scraps of wood you have in your shop, and the hardware is easy to find at any hardware store or home-improvement center.

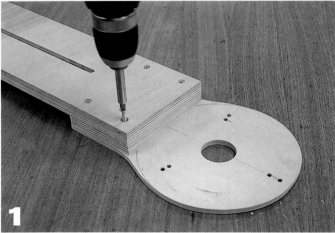

Shape the base plate to the general shape shown in the illustration. Make sure the base plate is large enough for your router base. Glue the spacer plate to the base plate. Then, using screws, attach this assembly to the arm plate.

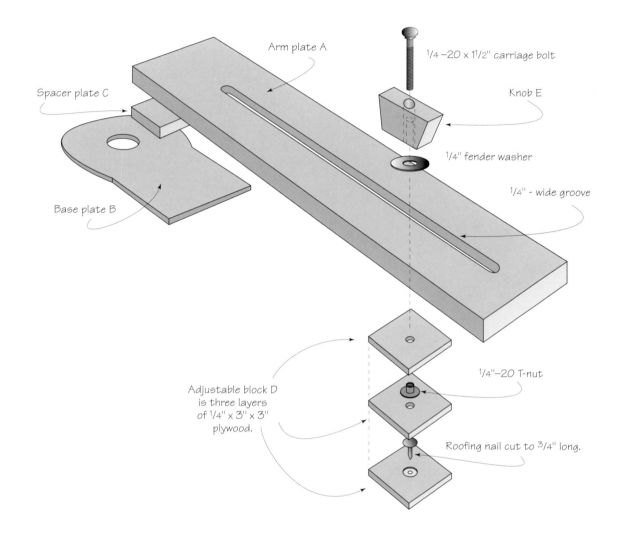

Arm plate A

Spacer plate C

Base plate B

$\frac{1}{4}$ –20 x $1\frac{1}{2}$" carriage bolt

Knob E

$\frac{1}{4}$" fender washer

$\frac{1}{4}$" - wide groove

Adjustable block D
is three layers
of $\frac{1}{4}$" x 3" x 3"
plywood.

$\frac{1}{4}$"–20 T-nut

Roofing nail cut to $\frac{3}{4}$" long.

MATERIALS LIST inches (millimeters)

REFERENCE	QUANTITY	PART	STOCK	THICKNESS	(mm)	WIDTH	(mm)	LENGTH	(mm)	COMMENTS
A	1	arm plate	plywood	$\frac{3}{4}$	(19)	5	(127)	20	(508)	
B	1	base plate	plywood	$\frac{1}{4}$	(6)	7	(178)	$10\frac{1}{2}$	(267)	
C	1	spacer plate	plywood	$\frac{1}{2}$	(13)	$3\frac{1}{2}$	(89)	5	(127)	
D	1	adjustable block	plywood	$\frac{3}{4}$	(19)	3	(76)	3	(76)	see step 2
E	1	knob	plywood	$\frac{3}{4}$	(19)	2	(51)	2	(51)	shape knob after drilling hole for T-nut

HARDWARE

1   $1\frac{1}{2}$" × $\frac{1}{4}$"–20 (38mm × 6mm–20) carriage bolt

1   $\frac{1}{4}$"–20 (6mm–20) T-nut

1   $\frac{1}{4}$" (6mm) fender washer

1   $1\frac{1}{4}$" (32mm) roofing nail (or any large-headed nail)

4   No. 8 × $1\frac{1}{4}$" (No. 8 × 32mm) wood screws

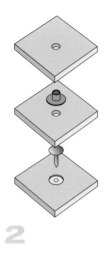

Drill a shallow counterbore in the bottom ¼"-thick plate to accept the nail head. This will allow the nail head to seat flush to the surface of the plate. Drill a pilot hole for the nail shank. Cut the nail ¾"-long and round the point. Insert the nail into the plate.

Drill a counterbore in the middle ¼"-thick plate to accept the head of the T-nut. Then drill the pilot hole for the barrel of the T-nut. Insert the T-nut into this plate. The head of the T-nut should be flush with the surface of the plate.

Drill a clearance hole for the bolt in the center ¼"-thick plate. Glue all three of the ¼"-thick adjustable plates together. Be careful not to get any glue in the threads of the T-nut.

Cut the knob to the shape shown in the illustration or choose your own shape. Counterbore for the T-nut and drill the through-hole for the bolt to pass through. Then soften the corners of the knob.

Remove the base plate on your router and use it as a drilling template to drill the screw holes into the base plate of the jig. Countersink for the base plate mounting screws and install the router base on the fixture base plate.

To use this jig, determine the radius you want to rout. With the router attached to the jig, measure from the inside of the router bit to the center of the nail in the adjustable block and tighten the adjustable block. Drill a pivot hole in your workpiece, insert the nail in the hole, and you're ready to rout.

routing a circle

This technique can be used to rout perfect circles if you don't own a band saw.

To make this jig, mill a strip of wood to the dimensions shown in the illustration. Make sure the strip slides easily in the miter groove in the router table's top. Drill a $\frac{1}{4}$"-diameter hole in the guide strip and glue the $\frac{1}{4}$"-diameter dowel in the hole.

Before using this router table setup, you should draw a circle on the material using a compass or trammel points. Drill a $\frac{1}{4}$"-diameter hole at the center of the circle about halfway through the material. Rough-cut the circle using a jigsaw. Then position the circle over the guide bar on the router table, centering it on the $\frac{1}{4}$"-diameter dowel attached to the guide bar. Move the guide bar toward the straight cutter in the router until the edge of the circle barely touches the cutter. Spin the circle to make sure no high spots will grab the cutter. When all is OK, clamp the guide bar to the router table and turn on the router. Carefully feed the circle against the cutter. If some low spots don't get cut, move the circle closer to the cutter and repeat the cutting. Do not remove more than $\frac{1}{16}$" of material at any one time when using this technique.

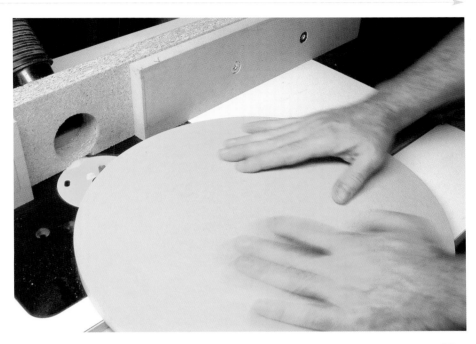

Draw the circle first, then drill a $\frac{1}{4}$"-diameter hole in the center of the circle. Finally, rough-cut the circle using a jigsaw.

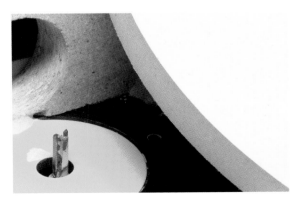

Using this technique, the edges of the disc are cleanly cut.

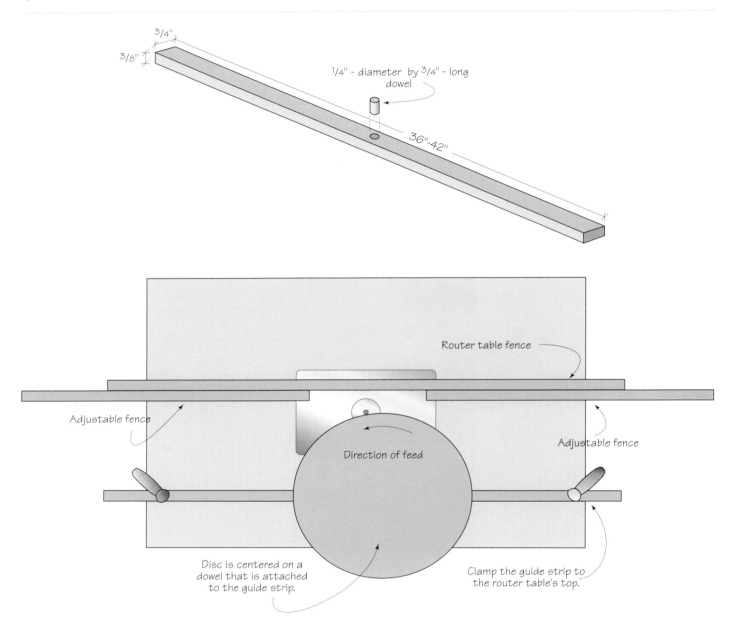

3/4"

3/8"

1/4" - diameter by 3/4" - long
dowel

36"-42"

Router table fence

Adjustable fence

Adjustable fence

Direction of feed

Disc is centered on a
dowel that is attached
to the guide strip.

Clamp the guide strip to
the router table's top.

jig for routing ellipses

An ellipse is an angled cross section of a cone and has constantly changing radii. This jig will enable you to cut patterns, grooves and templates. A perfect ellipse will be the result every time.

This jig can easily be sized larger. Determine how large your ellipse will be and cut the base plate to size. The grooves for the guide blocks will be the same size regardless of the base plate dimensions.

To begin, cut the base plate to size. Then set up a dado cutter in your table saw and cut the grooves for the guide blocks or cut the grooves using your router. Center the grooves on the base plate.

Cut out the pivot arm. Use a router mounted under a router table to cut the $\frac{1}{4}$" slot in the pivot arm. Next, cut out the guide blocks and drill them to accept the machine screws.

The mounting plate for the router that attaches to the pivot arm will vary in size and shape according to the size of your router.

Waxing the guide blocks and the guide block grooves will allow this jig to operate smoothly.

This jig can be adapted to rout small or large ellipse shapes. We used this basic principle in a production shop I worked in to make dozens of 5' by 7' conference tables.

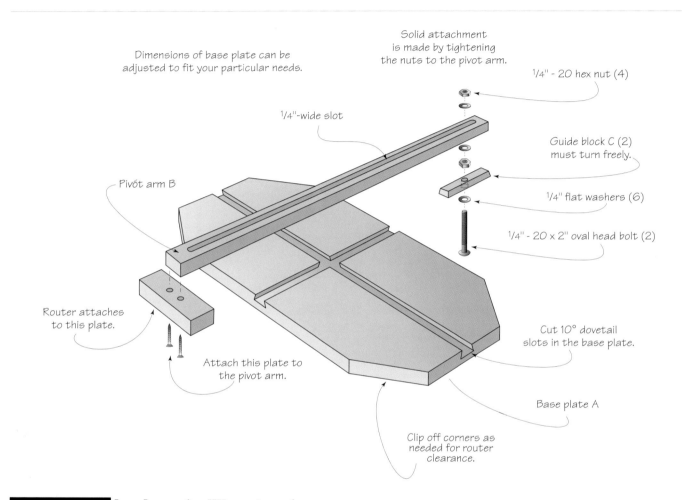

Dimensions of base plate can be adjusted to fit your particular needs.

Solid attachment is made by tightening the nuts to the pivot arm.

¹/₄" - 20 hex nut (4)

¹/₄"-wide slot

Guide block C (2) must turn freely.

Pivot arm B

¹/₄" flat washers (6)

¹/₄" - 20 x 2" oval head bolt (2)

Router attaches to this plate.

Cut 10° dovetail slots in the base plate.

Attach this plate to the pivot arm.

Base plate A

Clip off corners as needed for router clearance.

MATERIALS LIST inches (millimeters)

REFERENCE	QUANTITY	PART	STOCK	THICKNESS	(mm)	WIDTH	(mm)	LENGTH	(mm)	COMMENTS
A	1	base plate	plywood	³/₄	(19)	11	(279)	16	(406)	
B	1	pivot arm	hardwood	³/₄	(19)	1¹/₄	(32)	20	(508)	
C	2	guide blocks	hardwood	¹/₂	(13)	³/₄	(19)	3	(76)	
D	1	mounting plate	hardwood	¹/₂	(13)	³/₄	(19)	3	(76)	varies in size and shape according to the size of your router

HARDWARE

2	2" × ¹/₄"–20 (51mm × 6mm–20) ovalhead bolts
4	¹/₄"–20 (6mm–20) hex nuts
6	¹/₄" (6mm) flat washers
2	#8 × 1¹/₄" (32mm) drywall screws

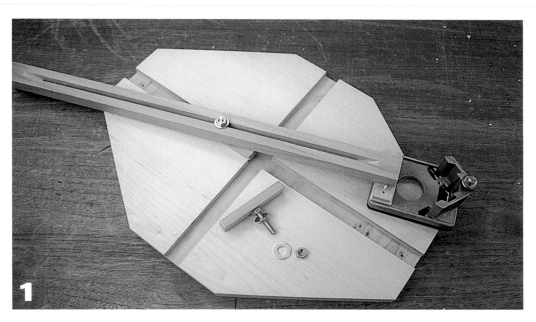

This photo shows the router base mounted to the pivot arm and one of the guide blocks, with all its parts. The mounting plate for the router will vary from router to router. The router base shown here is for a trim router.

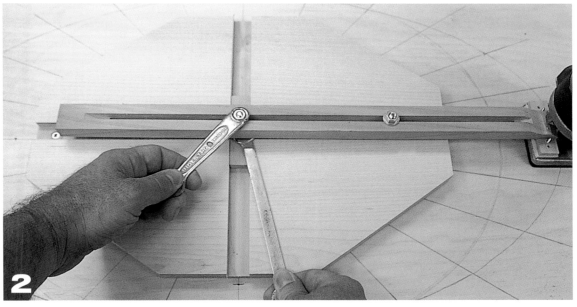

Draw the ellipse on the workpiece, center the jig on the ellipse and screw it in place. Attach the router to the pivot arm. Set the router on the longest point of the ellipse, locate the guide block that is the farthest away from the router in the center of the jig in the short groove. Tighten the nuts of the bolt to secure the block on the pivot arm (as shown in the photo). Use this procedure for the shortest point on the ellipse as well. Remember that the guide blocks need to be able to turn freely. Raise the router slowly, turn the router, lower the router into the workpiece and guide the router around the ellipse. If you've never used this type of jig before, make a few practice ellipses to get the feel of how the jig works.

self-centering router jig

This jig really does work! With a few scraps of plywood and some screws and washers, you can build this self-centering jig in 30 minutes or less.

Cut the parts as shown in the cutting list. Lay out the router base on the ¼" plywood and cut it to your desired shape. Remove the plastic from your router base and use it as a template to mark the center hole and screw holes on the plywood base.

It's important to have the router-base mounting holes located so they will center the router on the plywood base. Drill the screw holes as accurately as you can. Be sure to countersink the holes so the router-base mounting screw heads from your router will sit below the surface of the base. Drill the center router-bit clearance hole and glue the router base blocks in place as shown in the illustration.

Mark the holes in the ends of the end bars. Drill these holes large enough so the screws can be inserted in them with no force. The bars and the base will pivot on the screws through these holes.

Mark the pilot holes in the two side rails. Drill these holes and attach the end bars, but don't fully tighten the screws.

Mount the router to the plywood base. Then attach the plywood router base to the side rails.

This jig makes it easy to rout mortises exactly on center each and every time when dealing with different thicknesses of materials.

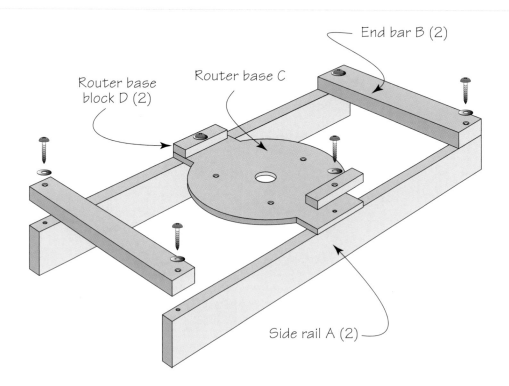

End bar B (2)

Router base C

Router base
block D (2)

Side rail A (2)

MATERIALS LIST inches (millimeters)

REFERENCE	QUANTITY	PART	STOCK	THICKNESS	(mm)	WIDTH	(mm)	LENGTH	(mm)
A	2	side rails	plywood	3/4	(19)	2	(51)	12	(305)
B	2	end bars	plywood	3/4	(19)	1	(25)	8	(203)
C	1	router base	plywood	1/4	(6)	8	(203)	8	(203)
D	2	router base blocks	plywood	1/2	(13)	3/4	(19)	2	(51)

HARDWARE

6   No. 8 × 1 1/2" (No. 8 x 38mm) roundhead wood screws

6   3/16" (5mm) flat washers

Lay out the desired shape of the router base, then cut it to shape using the band saw.

Be sure the holes that mount the base to the router hold the router in the center of the base. This will ensure the proper centering of the router in the jig. Drill a center hole just large enough to clear the bits you'll be using.

To use this jig, put it on the workpiece to be mortised or grooved and close the jig until both side rails are tight against the sides. Then, tighten the screws on the end bars and the plywood base. Slide the jig along the workpiece to cut the mortise.

■ *face-routing system*

A cabinet door, drawer front or side can be made from medium-density fiberboard (MDF) or a solid wood panel and given a raised-panel effect with a routed groove. This face-routing setup provides a system to guide the router and achieve a uniform margin on all four edges of the panel.

The system consists of four identical guides made of a base plate and an edge guide. The length of the guides should be as long as the part you plan to make.

Cut out all the parts and be sure the edge guides have one good straight edge.

Attach the guides to the base plates with nails or screws. Locate the guides at least 1" from the edges of the base plate.

When setting up the system, arrange the four guides like a pinwheel around the work. A flat work surface is the ideal place to set up this system. Be sure the guides on the base plates are close enough together so the router base plate will go into and out of the corners smoothly.

You are limited only by your imagination as to how you can use this system. The door being made in the photos is made in two steps. First, the profile is routed in the front of the door. Then the rabbet is routed in the back of the door. As the rabbet is completed, the panel will drop out.

Different-size router bases can be easily made on a stationary sander or band saw (see the illustration). These bases can be used to position the router in different locations on the door faces with reference to the guide rails.

This set up is totally flexible and quickly adjustable to different sizes of doors, drawer fronts and cabinet sides. With the interchangeable router bases, you can create patterns that you have only dreamed of.

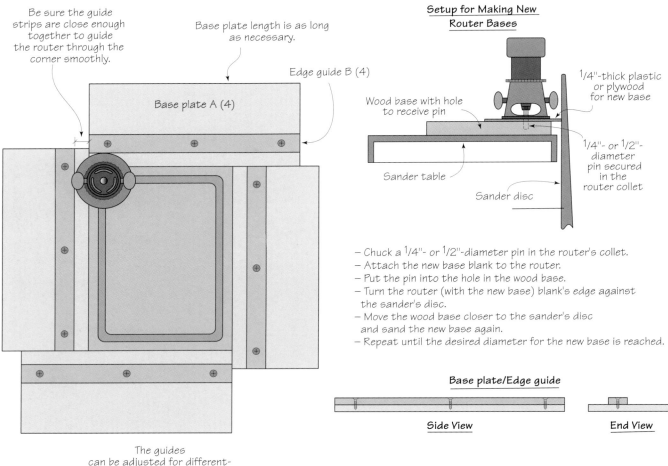

Be sure the guide strips are close enough together to guide the router through the corner smoothly.

Base plate length is as long as necessary.

Edge guide B (4)

Base plate A (4)

The guides can be adjusted for different-size doors by shifting the pinwheel setup.

Setup for Making New Router Bases

Wood base with hole to receive pin

1/4"-thick plastic or plywood for new base

1/4"- or 1/2"-diameter pin secured in the router collet

Sander table

Sander disc

– Chuck a 1/4"- or 1/2"-diameter pin in the router's collet.
– Attach the new base blank to the router.
– Put the pin into the hole in the wood base.
– Turn the router (with the new base) blank's edge against the sander's disc.
– Move the wood base closer to the sander's disc and sand the new base again.
– Repeat until the desired diameter for the new base is reached.

Base plate/Edge guide

Side View

End View

MATERIALS LIST inches (millimeters)

REFERENCE	QUANTITY	PART	STOCK	THICKNESS	(mm)	WIDTH	(mm)	LENGTH	(mm)	COMMENTS
A	4	base plates	MDF	3/4	(19)	6	(152)	24	(610)	length is as long as necessary
B	4	edge guides	MDF	3/4	(19)	2	(51)	24	(610)	length is as long as necessary

HARDWARE

16   No. 8 × 1 1/4" (32mm) flathead wood screws

Attach the guides with nails or screws.

A flat work top is ideal for using this system. The guide assemblies are screwed to the top.

When the second cut is made, the center panel will drop out and can be easily removed from the door.

This is a door that has been routed for a glass panel.

adjustable router base

This jig is simply an auxiliary router base with an adjustable fence for edging or cutting rabbets and dadoes. A support piece makes it possible to clamp the unit to a 2x4 sawhorse beam. It can also be clamped in a woodworker's vise. This provides a small portable router table that can be easily taken to the job site.

The beauty of the fence is that it requires only one end to be moved to adjust the distance from the bit to the fence. The range of that dimension is from flush to $4\frac{1}{2}$" (depending on the diameter of the bit). If needed, a second fence can be constructed. The second fence could be longer and permit the use of stop blocks. The base can easily be adapted to any common router base, including plunge routers.

Simplicity is the name of the game with this jig/fixture. It's versatility is great for working onsite. This is it — no need to carry around a router table. When it's used as a jig, you've got the fence to hang onto to guide the router safely.

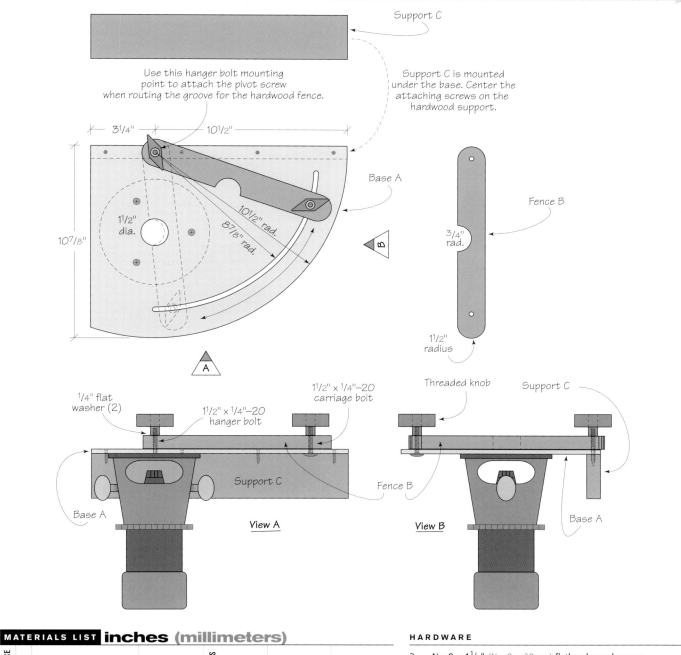

Support C

Use this hanger bolt mounting
point to attach the pivot screw
when routing the groove for the hardwood fence.

Support C is mounted
under the base. Center the
attaching screws on the
hardwood support.

3 1/4"   10 1/2"

Base A

1 1/2"
dia.

10 7/8"

10 1/2" rad.

8 7/8" rad.

B

Fence B

3/4"
rad.

1 1/2"
radius

A

1/4" flat
washer (2)

1 1/2" x 1/4"–20
hanger bolt

1 1/2" x 1/4"–20
carriage bolt

Threaded knob

Support C

Support C

Base A

View A

Fence B

View B

Base A

JIGS, FIXTURES & ACCESSORIES   **63**

MATERIALS LIST inches (millimeters)

REFERENCE	QUANTITY	PART	STOCK	THICKNESS	(mm)	WIDTH	(mm)	LENGTH	(mm)
A	1	base	plywood	1/4	(6)	10 7/8	(276)	14	(356)
B	1	fence	hardwood	3/4	(19)	1 1/2	(38)	10 7/8	(276)
C	1	support	hardwood	3/4	(19)	2 1/2	(64)	14	(356)

HARDWARE

3	No. 8 × 1 1/2" (No. 8 × 38mm) flathead wood screws
1	1 1/2" × 1/4"–20 (38mm × 6mm–20) carriage bolt
1	1 1/2" × 1/4"–20 (38mm × 6mm–20) hanger bolt
2	1/4"–20 (6mm–20) wing nuts or threaded knobs
2	1/4" (6mm) flat washers
4	No. 8 × 1 1/4"(32mm) drywall screws

1

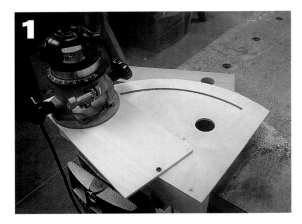

Cut the parts according to the cutting list. Attach the hardwood support to the base. Drill a router-cutter clearance hole in a scrap piece of wood. Center the router base over this hole and attach it to the scrap. Install a $\frac{1}{4}$" straight-cutting router bit in the router and attach the router to its base. Measure $8\frac{7}{8}$" from the edge of the router bit to the opposite end of the scrap wood and drill a pivot-screw hole. Attach this router assembly to the adjustable jig base at the point where the hanger bolt will be inserted (see illustration). Cut the groove for the fence. Install the hanger bolt, attach the hardwood fence, and you're ready to go.

Clamp the fixture in a vise or to a sawhorse and you're ready to start making grooves or whatever is needed.

This set up is ideal for routing rabbets or cutting profiles on mouldings.

Using the jig is safe and easy. The whole thing can be flipped over so you can guide the router over larger stock. This would be a good setup for profiling short-wall caps. The fence provides plenty of hand control.

routing a groove in a curved rail

When you make curved door or cabinet
panels that require curved rails, routing
the grooves for the panels is impossible
unless you use a router or cut them by
hand. Routing a groove in a curved rail is
similar to routing one in a straight rail.

Using a router table is the best way to
do this operation because the table will
support the rail throughout the entire cutting operation. Set the router table fence
so the straight-cutting router bit will be
located in the center of the rail. Set the
adjustable fences on the table fence so
they're about 2" apart. When the curved
rail is held against the fence, it will strad-
dle this gap. This will in turn steady the
rail as it's fed through the setup. Use a
featherboard to hold the rail snugly
against the fence so the rail doesn't wander
during the cutting of the groove.

It's better and safer to cut these grooves
in two or three passes, raising the router
bit a little each time. It's recommended
that you cut only ¼" deep at each pass.

A straight-cutting bit, a feather board and a router table work well to cut a groove in a
curved rail. As always, make test cuts in scrap wood until you get the feel for this operation.
Make several shallow cuts rather than one deep one.

The router will cut clean grooves everytime. The tenons on this rail could have been cut using a straight-cutting bit using the same basic setup used here.

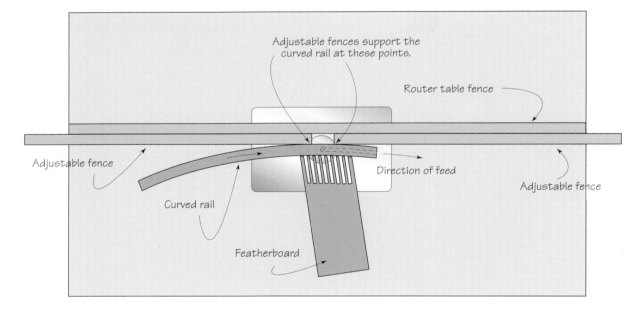

Adjustable fences support the curved rail at these points.

Router table fence

Adjustable fence

Direction of feed

Adjustable fence

Curved rail

Featherboard

■ *routing a cavity*

Sometimes you need to remove material from the middle of a blank of wood. If it's a small blank, the router table is the perfect tool to use. Stop blocks can be used to define the area of the cavity. A straight-cutting bit in a router will perform the task of material removal. Continue raising the router bit until the desired depth of the cavity is reached.

If the cavity to be created is large — for example, a space that will hold a chopping block in a kitchen countertop — a jig can made that will guide the router. When using this jig, the same rule of making shallow cuts applies. Trying to remove too much material at one time could result in a broken router bit, or torn or ragged cuts in the wood, or the router being knocked out of control or twisted from your hands.

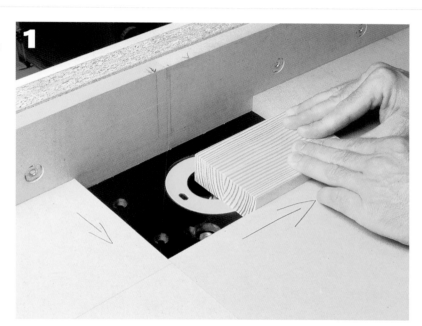

After setting the stop blocks, raise the router bit so it cuts about 1/8"-deep. Holding the wooden blank against the lower right-hand corner of the stop blocks, lower it down on the spinning router bit. Holding the blank against the stop blocks, move the blank toward the fence, holding it against the right stop. Then, move the blank to the left, then toward your body and finally to the right.

Make shallow cuts to create the cavity. Raise the router bit in 1/8" increments and repeat the routing process.

Keep raising the router bit until you've reached the desired depth of the cavity.

Set up the router table fence and use the same straight-cutting bit to cut rabbets on the inside edges of the lid. Soften the corners with sandpaper and you've made a box on the router table!

routing a mortise for a lock

Mortised locks, and some door catches, need to be set into a mortise. Usually a mounting plate will hold the lock or catch in place. Routing a shallow mortise for the mounting plate will give a nice, clean look to the lock when it's installed.

To rout this mortise, first draw layout lines showing the location of the mortise. Usually, the mounting plate is a standard width: $\frac{1}{4}$", $\frac{3}{8}$" or $\frac{1}{2}$". Choose the correct size router bit and install it in the router. Use a fence mounted on the router base to guide the router when cutting the mortise. Set the fence so the mortise is cut in the center of the material. Set the depth of the cut and you're good to go. The mortise for the mounting plates is shallow, so one cut should work.

The deeper part of the mortise that houses the workings of the lock or catch can be routed or drilled out. A chisel can be used for the final fitting of the mortise if necessary.

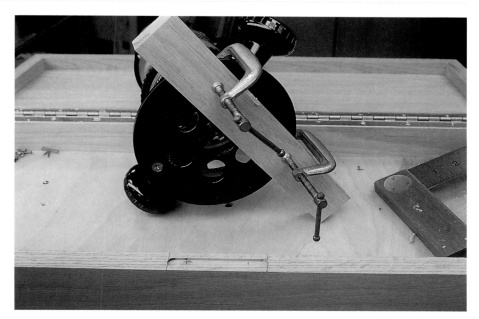

If your router didn't come with a fence attachment, you can improvise a fence using a scrap of wood and two clamps. Use a hammer to fine tune the adjustment of the fence. Double-check to be sure the clamps are snug and start routing.

routing a rabbet for a continuous hinge

To install a continuous hinge quickly and easily, you can rout a rabbet that is as deep as the thickness of the closed hinge. To rout this rabbet, you can use a rabbeting bit or you can attach a fence to your router and cut it that way. The advantage of using the fence is that the fence and the base of the router create a right angle that supports the cut after the material has been removed.

After you have cut the rabbet, cut the corners of the rabbet square and install the hinge.

This is my two-cent fence. I wanted washers that were wide but I only had small holes for the screws, so pennies came to the rescue. For smaller routing jobs like this, a trim router works great. Set the fence and make some test cuts in scrap wood to get a feel for this setup. It may take a couple of practice runs to get accustomed to holding the router squarely to the edge of the part once some of the material has been removed. Learning to use the router is like learning to use any hand tool. It takes some practice to get the right feel and gain confidence.

routing a cabinet handle

This technique is a safe way to make narrow, moulded parts. Start with stock that is twice as wide (plus the width of a saw kerf) as the finished parts. Rout the desired profile on both edges of the stock.

The idea shown here was used to create door pulls. The profile was routed first, then the parts were separated using the table saw.

For the final profile, a straight-cutting bit was installed in the router, and a stop block was set up to define the length of the cut and to support the stock when this first plunge cut was made. Start the cut by resting the end of the stock against the stop block and holding the remaining stock away from the cutter. Feed the stock into the cutter while holding it against the stop block. This is a safe operation and shouldn't be feared. Complete the cut by feeding the stock through the cutter.

The solution to the problem of narrow door stock was to add a full-length handle to each door. The router table and a couple of router bits came to the rescue.

This is the safe way to cut profiles on parts that would be too small to safely feed through the cutter.

2

Separate the profiled parts using a table saw or band saw.

3

Set up a stop block on the router table fence. To start the cut, rest the end of the material against the stop block while holding the stock away from the cutter. Push the stock into the cutter and complete the cut by running the stock along the fence through the cutter.

template routing

Using templates to rout and shape multiple parts is one of the jobs a router was made to do. You can make templates for creating all kinds of shapes. You're limited only by your imagination. These templates will never change and can be used again and again, for years on end, if you do production work.

The recommended material for making templates is void-free plywood. Baltic birch is the best. Plywood is stable by design and will not expand or contract with the change of seasons, and grain direction is not a concern. Any shape can be cut to maximize material usage with no worries.

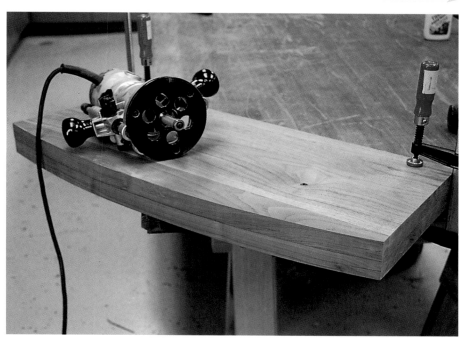

This is one way of template routing. Make the first part with the proper pattern, then use the first part as a template for routing the other parts. These parts are the top and bottom of a cabinet, and they needed to be exactly the same shape and size.

Using a router bit with a guide bearing on the shank of the bit is easy. Make the template of the pattern you want, attach it to the workpiece and rout. These bits are great for routing holes of any shape because you don't need to account for the diameter of a routing collar and bit diameter. Simply cut the hole to the exact size in the template, attach it to the workpiece, rout and you're done.

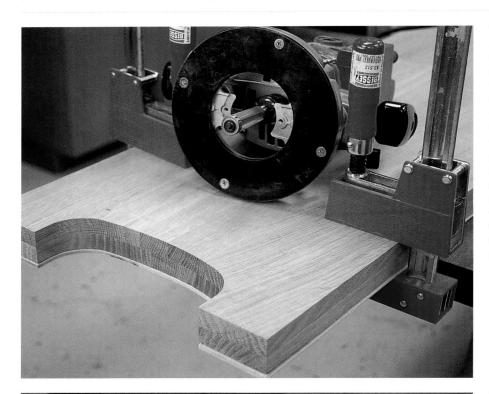

When you want to rout a certain pattern on a work-piece, make the pattern or template out of plywood or MDF. These materials are stable and won't change shape if you want to reuse the template a year later. Take your time and cut the shape in the template exactly as you would like the final pattern to look. Make sure there are no bumps or other un-wanted variations in the template as these will be transferred to the final workpiece. Using the tem-plate as a pattern, draw the shape on the work-piece and use a jigsaw or band saw to cut away all of the waste material up to an $\frac{1}{8}$" away from the drawing line. Then set up the template on the workpiece, securing it in place. Using a flush-trimming router bit, let the guide bearing run along the edge of the template to complete the pattern on the workpiece.

If you're making multiple parts, it's easier to mount aligning strips on the routing template to hold the parts. Secure the template to a work surface and insert the rough-cut parts into the template. Rout the pattern and move on to the next part. Note that these parts were held in place by screws inserted into the ends of the part. The holes were hidden once the parts were put into place on the project. If only the fronts of the parts had been showing, they could have been held in place with screws inserted from the bottom of the template.

■ *routing dovetails*

The dovetail routing jig has been available for several years and is made by several different manufacturers. It's still a great jig to use to cut dovetails. These are half-blind dovetails, which means you can't see the ends of the tails when the joint is assembled.

We used this same style of jig in commercial shops for years because it cuts consistently clean and tightly fitting dovetails. The joints look like they were cut with a machine, and that's what they are — machine-cut dovetails that create a strong joint. Don't let anyone tell you this jig isn't worth the time it takes to set it up. You'll be pleased time and time again as you use this jig.

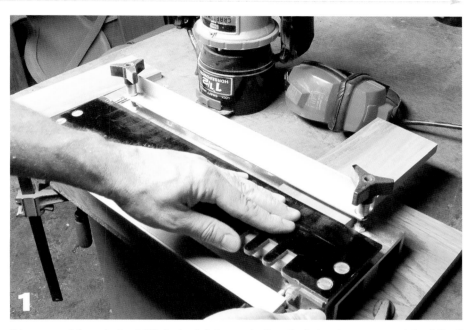

This commercially made dovetail jig is simple but accurate. Once the jig is set up, you can cut dovetails all day long with consistently good results. I attached mine to a scrap of plywood. I drilled a hole in the plywood so I can hang the jig on the wall when it's not in use. The plywood also allows the jig to be secured to a workbench top with clamps. Set up the jig by adjusting the finger template height to the thickness of the stock. Note the 20-year-old router behind the jig. I've only used this router for cutting dovetails with this jig. I never change the setup, so it's always ready to go whenever I need it.

Use the finger template to register the end of the part that will have the tails. The top edge of the part is located toward the outside of the jig and rests against a registering pin. The inside of the part faces out toward the operator.

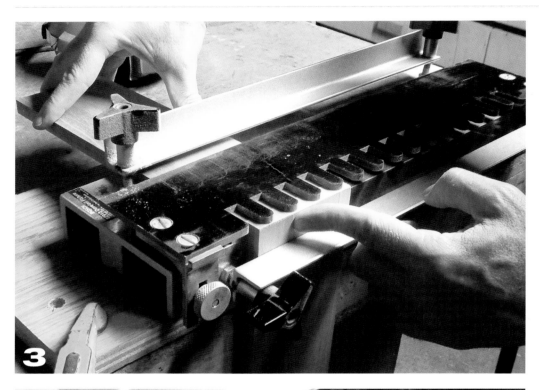

After tightening the hold-down for the tail stock, use it to register the end of the socket part. Tighten the hold-down for the socket part. The top edge of the socket part is pointed toward the outside of the jig and registers against a pin. The inside of this part faces up. These pins (preset at the factory) create the proper offset so both parts can be routed at the same time.

Double-check to be sure all the hold-downs are tight and the parts are securely held in place. Make the first cut with the router by resting the router base on the finger template and making a scoring cut on the face of the tail part. Make this cut by running the router from right to left. This is the reverse of the proper feed direction for the router so make this a light cut. This cut will prevent the wood from tearing out when you run the router from left to right as you follow the finger template with the router.

Fitting Dovetails

If the tails are too tight, lower the height (relative to the router base) of the dovetail bit just a little (use $1/64$" increments) at a time until the fit is snug. Conversely, if the tails are too loose, raise the height of the bit.

Make the second cut from left to right, following the template. (A rub collar is attached to the router base and follows the finger template.)

This jig will cut clean joints like this time after time when the dovetail bit is sharp.

If you're making drawer parts, cut all the dovetails first, then cut the grooves for the drawer bottom. Cut the groove so it's located in the middle of a socket and pin. When the joint is assembled, the end of the groove will be hidden by the half-blind socket.

You should need only light hammer blows to assemble the joint.

jointing on the router table

Using a straight-cutting carbide router bit, you can cut a straight edge on almost any material. Wood, nonferrous sheets of metal, high-pressure laminate, particleboard and MDF can all be straight cut. Think of this setup as a jointer sitting on edge. The only thing to remember is to take shallow cuts. I recommend no more than $\frac{1}{16}$" or 2mm at a time.

I used to have a small router table set up just for jointing the edges of high-pressure laminate. I did a lot of inlay work and once the edges were jointed, the seams were perfect.

The router table can be used as a jointer with awesome results. A piece of stiff cardboard or high-pressure laminate is used to offset the face of the outfeed fence relative to the infeed fence. This offset should be no more than $\frac{1}{16}$". Use a straight-cutting bit with a screwed cutter. This will slice rather than just cut the wood and will leave an incredibly smooth surface. This router bit just happened to have a guide bearing, but it's not used for the jointing operation.

It may take a few passes to straighten a rough or uneven edge, but this is just as good as a real jointer.

mortising jig for a butt hinge

This jig is made of three pieces of scrap wood and can be dimensioned for butt hinges of any size. The template is a piece of plywood with a cutout sized to guide the router to make a mortise the same length as the hinge's leaf.

You can configure this jig in many ways. If you have a straight-cutting router bit with a guide bearing on the shaft, make a cutout in a ¾"-thick scrap of plywood the same size as the hinge's leaf. Then make two cleats that are ¾"-thick by 1½"-wide and are 3" to 4" longer than the plywood template.

A second way is to use a straight-cutting router bit in combination with a guide bushing mounted in the router base. Make the cutout in the plywood the length of the hinge's leaf plus the diameter of the guide bushing minus the diameter of the router bit.

A third way is to use a straight-cutting router bit in combination with the router's base. Make the cutout in the plywood the same length as the hinge's leaf plus the width or diameter of the router's base minus the diameter of the router bit. If you have a trimmer router, this is a good application for it. The entire base of the average trimmer router is about 3" square. This means it is possible to use the router without a guide bushing. The whole base of the router can be used as a guide in the cutout on the template.

Clamp the cleats to opposite faces of the workpiece with the edges of the cleats flush with the edge of the workpiece. The workpiece should be facing toward you. Lay the template on top of this and attach it to the cleats. The mortise is cut from the front toward the back of the workpiece and is the same width and length as the hinge's leaf. You want the barrel of the hinge to remain proud of the front face of the workpiece.

The depth of the mortise is regulated by the depth of the cut you make with the router bit. After you've cut a mortise using the jig, the jig will be easy to align where you've marked the hinge location. The router will have cut into the front cleat the same width and depth as the mortise.

Depending on the style of the hinge's leaves, you may need to square the corners of the mortise.

flush-trimming guide fence

This fence is an attachment that can be made for the router table. Cut a ¾"-thick fence strip 4"-wide and 36"-long. Cut a ¼"-wide groove ⅜"-deep in the fence strip and center it ⅜" from the bottom edge. Cut two guide strips ¼"-thick by 1"-wide and 17"-long. Glue these into the groove in the fence strip, leaving a ¾" gap between their ends at the center of the fence strip.

When the glue dries, the flush-trimming guide fence is ready to use. Clamp it to the main fence on the router table, centering the gap between the strips around a straight-cutting router bit. Set the fence so the edges of the guide strips are flush with the outside edge of the router bit.

When the edge of the veneered panel is run along the guide strips, the veneer hanging over the guide strips will be trimmed flush with the edge of the panel.

This flush-trimming guide fence will work for both one-sided and two-sided veneered panels.

routing a rabbet

Rabbet-cutting bits have cutters that are set and sharpened on a bias, so the cutter slices rather than chops the wood. A rabbet-cutting router bit has several different sized guide bearings that can guide the router bit. Depending on the diameter of the guide bearing, different depths of rabbets can be cut. This photo shows a rabbet-cutting bit being used to cut a rabbet in the back inside edge of a side panel for a cabinet. This rabbet will house the back panel of the cabinet.

After a picture or door frame has been assembled, a rabbet can be cut on the inside of the frame for holding a mirror, glass or wooden panel. After you've routed the rabbet, use a chisel to square out the corners of the rabbet.

router bit guide bearings

This is one of the most common uses of a router. Most router bits that cut a profile have guide bearings. These router bits can be used in the router table or used while holding and guiding the router. Whether the part is straight or curved, router bits with guide bearings can be used to shape the edges of your work. Sometimes it's better to custom-make a base for the router that is larger than the standard base. There can be two reasons for doing this. First, the router bit may cut a larger radius than the stock router base center hole. You can cut whatever size center hole is necessary to clear the router bit cutter. Second, the larger base will give you better support for the router by providing a larger contact surface with the workpiece.

routing a groove

In Europe, I know it's not permitted to use dado heads or other types of cutters in table saws. Cutting grooves with the router is the best solution. By it's very name, a router is meant to cut grooves.

Straight and curved grooves are no problem for the router. Straight-edged or curved-edged templates are all that's needed. As shown in the photos, the router base can be used to reference the cut or a guide collar could be used. With either method, the distance from the edge of the router bit to the edge of the guide needs to be known. Use this measurement to locate the routing template when setting up to rout a groove.

Mark where you want the groove. Measure the distance (d) from the edge of the router bit to the edge of the router's base.

Use the distance (d) to set the guide fence from the edge of the groove.

Set the router on the workpiece and run the router against the guide fence. If you're standing with the guide fence on your left, feed the router forward against the guide fence. This will ensure that the router stays against the guide fence. If you run the router the opposite direction, it will pull away from the guide fence and be pulled into the workpiece. If you haven't used the router like this before, practice on scrap wood before cutting into your workpiece.

This is what the router does best — it cuts clean grooves each and every time.

■ jig for cutting a mortise

This jig is made the same way as the mortising jig for a butt hinge. A piece of scrap plywood and two cleats are all that's needed. If you're using a straight-cutting router bit with a guide bearing on the shaft, the cutout in the plywood template is the same size as the finished mortise. If you're using a guide bushing, the cutout is the same size as the mortise plus the diameter of the bushing minus the diameter of the router bit. This applies to both the length and width of the cutout.

To make the jig, attach the cleats to the workpiece so the edges of the cleats are flush with the edges of the workpiece. Attach the template so the mortise will be located in the desired position relative to the width of the workpiece. The location of the mortise along the length of the workpiece can be set wherever you put the jig.

2

A plunge router is the best choice for cutting mortises. You locate the router on the jig and lower the bit into the workpiece.

3

A router-cut mortise is clean and precise.

European cup-hole template

This template can be used to rout perfectly sized 35mm cup holes for European hinges. If you use this type of hinge only occasionally, this is the way to go to avoid buying a 35mm Forstner bit that you'll use sparingly.

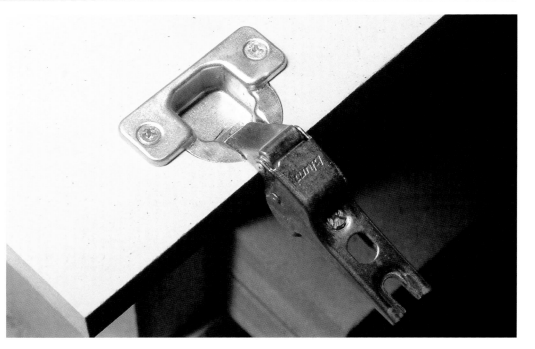

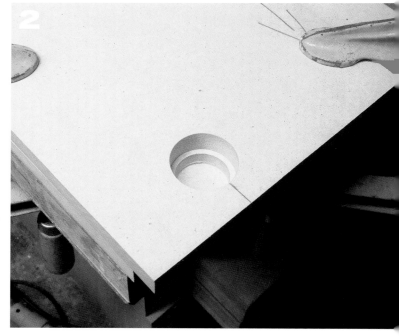

To make this template, decide what guide bushing and router bit combination you'll use each time you rout these cup holes. To determine the diameter of the template hole, add 35mm plus the diameter of the guide bushing in millimeters minus the diameter of the router bit in millimeters.

The finished cup hole will be 35mm in diameter and 13mm deep.

hole routing template

If you want to drill super clean-cut holes, this is the template to use. It's perfect for drilling holes in plywood veneer where a normal drill bit would tear out the wood fibers or in high-pressure laminate-covered panels. The high-pressure laminate can dull drill bits quickly whereas a carbide router bit will drill hundreds of holes without a wimper.

As you did for the European cup-hole template, determine what combination of guide bushing and router bit you'll be using with this template. If you want to bore a 5mm diameter hole (a standard size for using the European 32mm system of cabinet hardware), add 5mm plus the diameter of the guide bushing in millimeters minus the diameter of the router bit in millimeters. This is the diameter of the hole to drill in the template. If you space the holes 32mm on center, you're good to go for making cabinets using the European drawer slide and hinges.

game table

THIS GAME TABLE IS BASED ON THE ellipse and its curves and is a perfect project to make using the router. The only two straight lines are the center lines of the game board. You'll be using the ellipse routing jig for this project. Making this table will require some patience, but the results are worth it.

I created the curves of the game board by drawing the table top outline and placing concentric ellipses that were progressively 4" narrower inside of the first ellipse with the lengths of all the ellipses remaining the same. I ended with a straight line down the center of the ellipses. Then I copied this pattern, turned it 90° and centered it on the first layout. The lines were truncated at the outside intersections where the eight-by-eight "square" game board was created.

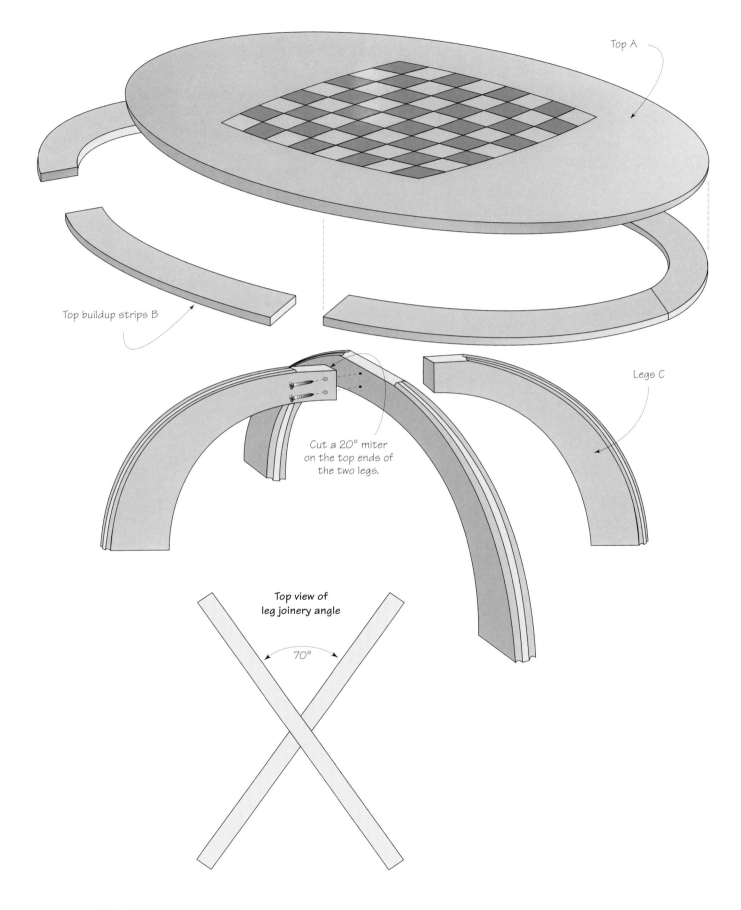

Top A

Top buildup strips B

Legs C

Cut a 20° miter
on the top ends of
the two legs.

**Top view of
leg joinery angle**

70°

REFERENCE	QUANTITY	PART	STOCK	THICKNESS	(mm)	WIDTH	(mm)	LENGTH	(mm)	COMMENTS
A	1	top	MDF	³/₄	(19)	24	(610)	36	(914)	
B		top buildup strips	MDF	³/₄	(19)	4	(102)			lay out the strips on scrap material; number is as many as required
C	4	leg blanks	MDF	³/₄	(19)	14	(356)	28	(711)	glue two pieces together to make 1¹/₂" (38mm) -thick leg blanks
D	1	mounting plate	MDF	³/₄	(19)	14	(356)	26	(660)	

HARDWARE

4	No. 8 × 2" (50mm) wood screws
4	No. 8 × 1¹/₄" (30mm) wood screws
4	metal or nylon furniture glides
1	12 oz. (340g) can of dark paint for game top
1	12 oz. (340g) can of light paint for game top
2	12 oz. (340g) cans of textured color
	Deft Clear Wood Finish, gloss

Leg Pattern

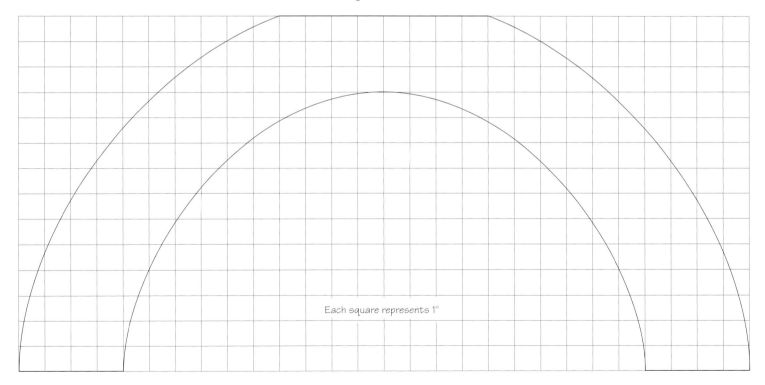

Each square represents 1"

Game Board Pattern

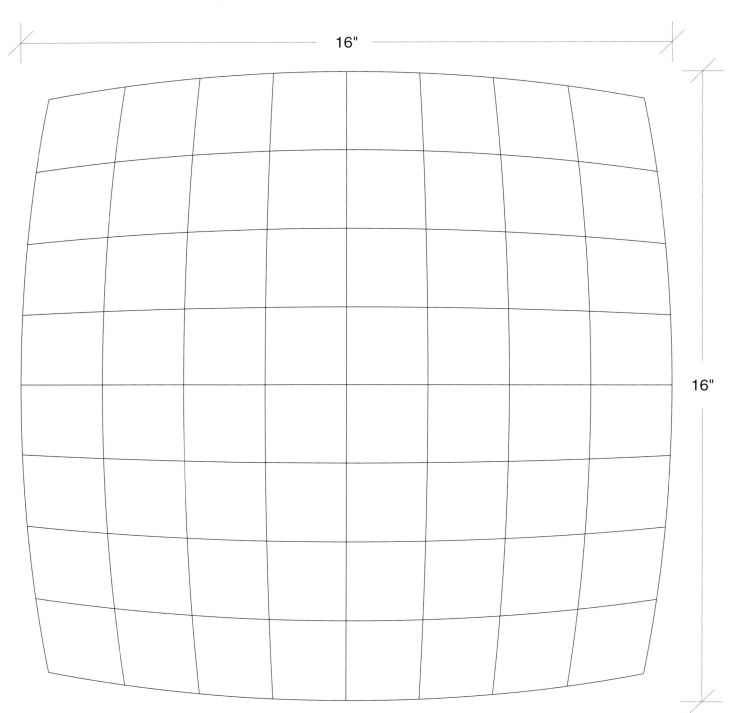

16"

16"

Use the pattern illustration as a guide to create a full-size leg pattern. Draw the pattern on paper and use spray adhesive to attach it to some scrap wood. Cut out the pattern and sand it until the curves are smooth. Trace the pattern onto the glued-up leg blanks. Cut out the legs about ¹/₈" outside the pattern lines.

After you've cut out the legs, attach the leg pattern to the rough-cut legs. Set up a flush-trimming router bit in a router table. The bearing on the bit will rub against the leg pattern and cut the leg identical to the leg pattern. If you have a long flush-trimming router bit, you can make this cut in one pass.

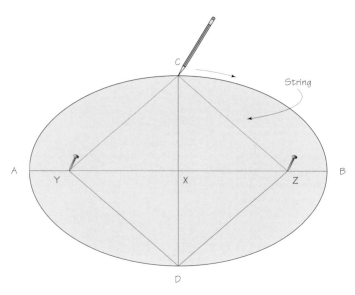

Use the nail, string and pencil method to draw the shape of the tabletop on the tabletop blank. Then rough-cut the top to shape about ¹/₂" outside the line of the tabletop. Using screws, attach the ellipse-routing jig to the bottom of the tabletop. Leave the guide blocks slightly loose on the arm of the jig. Insert the guide blocks into the grooves in the jig and set the router (with the bit already installed in the router) at the width and height lines of the tabletop shape. Tighten the blocks. This sets the jig to guide the router. Start the router and make the cut.

To draw an ellipse, all you need is a compass, two nails and a piece of string. Start by drawing two lines, AB and CD, perpendicular to each other and intersecting at their centers. AD is the final length and CD is the final width of the ellipse. Set your compass to AX and hold the tip at D. Strike an arc at Y and Z on AB. Put the nails at Y and Z. Tie the string in a loop, holding it tight between Y, C (where you are holding your pencil) and Z. Keep the string tight as you draw the ellipse.

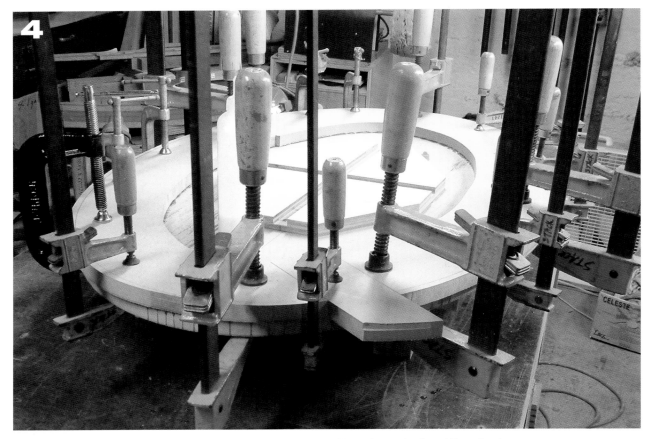

4

In order to add some visual and physical thickness to the tabletop, some buildup strips need to be cut. Trace the shape of the tabletop onto some scrap pieces of wood. Some of the falloff pieces from the table will work nicely. Cut these strips to the rough shape of the top. Then, 4" in from the rough cuts you've just made, draw a parallel line. This will roughly define the inside radii of the strips. Cut on these lines. Then, glue these buildup strips to the bottom of the top.

5

After the glue has dried, set up a flush-trimming bit in the router and trim the buildup strips flush with the outside edges of the tabletop. Then, round over the inside edges of the buildup strips with a $\frac{1}{4}$" or $\frac{3}{8}$" roundover bit.

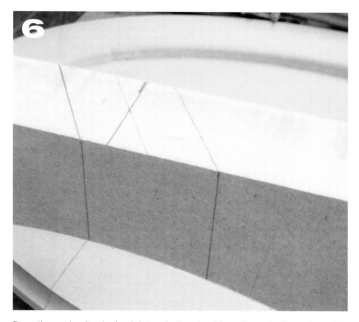

Draw the angles for the leg joint on both sets of legs. Draw the lines down the sides of the legs so you'll have guide lines for separating the legs on one set and attaching these legs to the other set. Then rout the coves on all curved edges of the legs. Leave the straight, top edges untouched. Rout the coves on the top and bottom of the outside edge of the tabletop.

Set the legs against the fence of your miter saw and clamp them in place. Set the saw tilt to 20°.

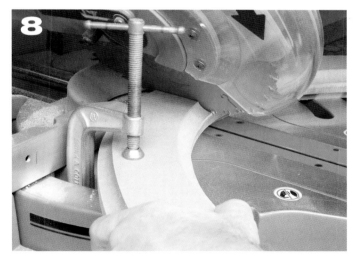

Make the cut to separate the first leg. Move the leg and clamp it into place and make the second cut. What you've done is cut out the material where the other set of legs will intersect these separated legs.

Glue and screw the separated legs to the other set of legs. This turned out to be a very strong butt joint.

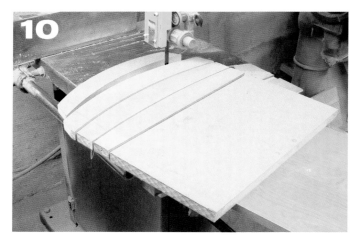

When cutting the templates for routing the grooves for the game table, cut them from the same piece of wood. Move the pin for each successive cut. The kerf of the band saw blade is so narrow that it doesn't affect the radius as each template is set against the next one in the game table groove routing template.

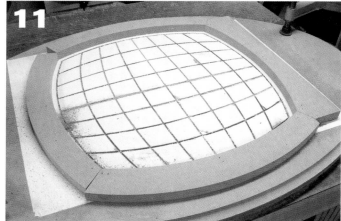

This is the part of building this game table that requires some patience on the part of the builder. It's not difficult but it does require some precision in setup and execution. To start the routing process, cut four templates at the outside radius of the game board and attach them to the tabletop. These need to be located squarely in the center of the top. All the rest of the routing is based on these templates.

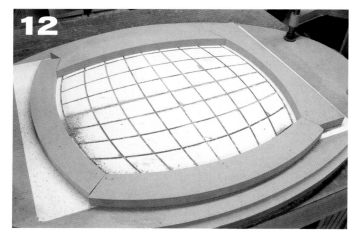

After routing the outside lines of the game board, cut the next template and put it against the outside template. Rout the next groove. Move this template to each of the four sides.

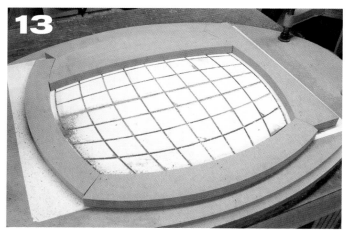

Cut the next template. Keep the first template and locate this template against it. Move both templates for each groove as in step 13.

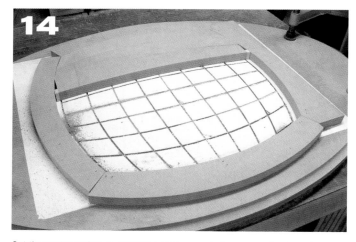

Cut the next template and rout the grooves as in the proceeding two steps.

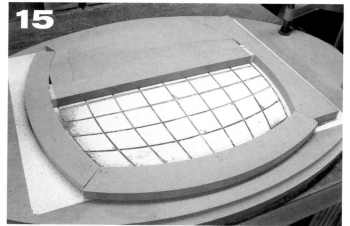

The last template will be a straight groove and you'll only need to rout two grooves 90° to each other in the center of the game board.

Cut the mounting plate for the legs. This is a smaller ellipse that fits inside the buildup strips on the underside of the tabletop. This plate can be cut out freehand using a band saw or jigsaw. Round over the edges using a $\frac{3}{8}$" roundover bit. Sand the parts, paying special attention to the edges. Be sure to sand them as smooth as the flat surfaces. Finish the table (see "Finishing the Game Table" sidebar).

■ FINISHING THE GAME TABLE

After the game board is routed into the tabletop, the grooves can be filled with colored car body filler (as I did) or inlaid with wood veneer.

After filling (or inlaying), mask off all the grooves with pin-striping tape and apply the first game board color. It doesn't matter which color you apply first. It's best to spray the paint so you don't have to deal with brush marks. Apply light coats of paint until the paint levels out smoothly. Let this paint dry for two or three days. Then, mask off every other "square" and apply the second color of paint. After this paint is level and smooth, let it dry for two or three days.

Remove all the masking tape and spray the game board with five coats of clear lacquer. Before you do this, make a sample board with the two game board colors applied to it. Apply the clear lacquer to this board. Be sure the paint doesn't react with the lacquer. I recommend that you use Deft Clear Wood Finish in the gloss finish. I know other types of lacquers are harder, but they will probably bubble or wrinkle the paint. Allow the first five coats of lacquer to dry and shrink for one week. Using 600-grit wet/dry sandpaper, wet sand the lacquer to flatten it. Use mineral spirits as the wet sanding lubricant. Then apply 10 more coats of clear lacquer. After one week of drying and curing, wet sand again. Buff the finish with #0000 steel wool. Apply a coat of paste wax.

Finally, mask off the game board. I applied a textured, granite-looking finish to the tabletop and the legs. I painted the mounting plate a neutral color with no texturing. Allow this finish one or two days to dry. Seal this finish with two coats of clear lacquer. Remove the masking tape, attach the legs and you're ready to play a game of checkers or chess.

After the table is finished, attach the mounting plate to the legs with screws.

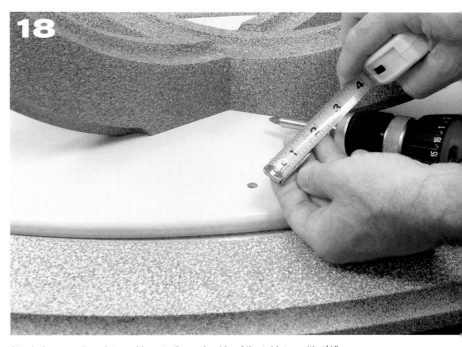

Attach the mounting plate and legs to the underside of the tabletop with $1\frac{1}{4}$" screws. Triple-check the length of these screws. You don't want to have them come through the top of the game table! Install the furniture glides on the "feet" of the legs.

showcase cabinet

THIS SHOWCASE CABINET IS THE opposite of the game table in its concept and design. I decided to make all the lines straight. No curves or rounded edges. This led to a complex cabinet with every edge beveled, even if the bevel was only $\frac{1}{16}$" wide.

The cabinet was constructed using mortise-and-tenon joinery. The cabinet box was constructed first, then the mortises were cut in the legs so they aligned with the tenons on the box.

The legs were tapered on the jointer, but they could have been tapered on the router table using an offset outfeed fence.

The cabinet is finished with three coats of rub-on polyurethane/oil finish.

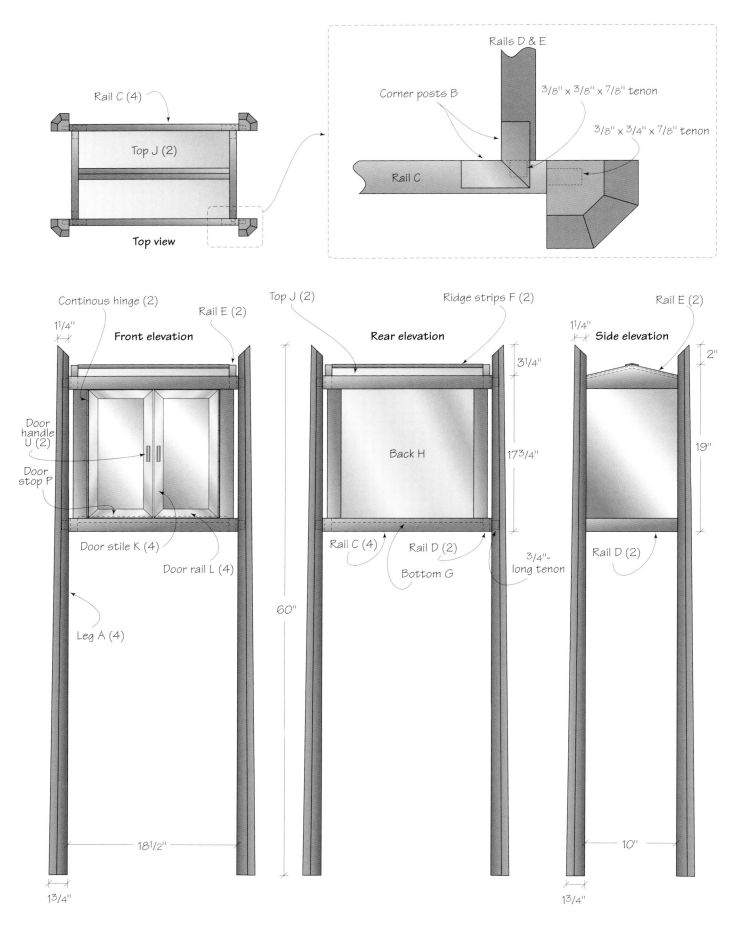

Rail C (4)

Top J (2)

Top view

Rails D & E

Corner posts B

3/8" x 3/8" x 7/8" tenon

3/8" x 3/4" x 7/8" tenon

Rail C

Continous hinge (2)

Rail E (2)

Top J (2)

Ridge strips F (2)

Rail E (2)

1 1/4"

Front elevation

Rear elevation

1 1/4"

Side elevation

2"

3 1/4"

Door
handle
U (2)

Door
stop P

Back H

17 3/4"

19"

Door stile K (4)

Door rail L (4)

Leg A (4)

Rail C (4)

Rail D (2)

Bottom G

3/4"-
long tenon

Rail D (2)

60"

18 1/2"

10"

1 3/4"

1 3/4"

REFERENCE	QUANTITY	PART	STOCK	THICKNESS	(mm)	WIDTH	(mm)	LENGTH	(mm)	COMMENTS
A	4	legs	padauk	$1^3/_4$	(45)	$1^3/_4$	(45)	60	(1524)	
B	8	corner posts	wenge	$5/_8$	(16)	$1^1/_2$	(38)	$14^3/_4$	(375)	cut 45° bevel on one long edge
C	4	rails	wenge	$3/_4$	(19)	$1^1/_2$	(38)	20	(508)	$3/_8$ x $3/_4$ x $7/_8$ (10mm x 19mm x 22mm) tenon both ends
D	2	rails	wenge	$3/_4$	(19)	$1^1/_2$	(38)	$10^3/_4$	(273)	$1/_4$ x $3/_8$ x $7/_8$ (6mm x 10mm x 22mm) tenon both ends
E	2	rails	wenge	$3/_4$	(19)	$2^3/_4$	(70)	$10^3/_4$	(273)	$1/_4$ x $3/_8$ x $7/_8$ (6mm x 10mm x 22mm) tenon both ends
F	2	ridge strips	wenge	$1/_4$	(6)	$3/_4$	(19)	$16^1/_2$	(419)	cut 13° - 14° bevel on one long edge
G	1	bottom	plywood	$1/_2$	(13)	10	(254)	$16^1/_2$	(419)	bird's eye maple veneer plywood
H	1	back	plywood	$1/_2$	(13)	$14^3/_4$	(375)	$16^1/_2$	(419)	bird's eye maple veneer plywood
J	2	tops	plywood	$1/_2$	(13)	$5^1/_8$+/-	(130)	$16^1/_2$	(419)	cut 13° - 14° bevel one long edge, bird's eye maple veneer, fit to width
K	4	door stiles	maple	$11/_{16}$	(17)	1	(25)	$14^5/_8$	(371)	45° miter both ends
L	4	door rails	maple	$11/_{16}$	(17)	1	(25)	7+/-	(178)	45° miter both ends
M	4	glass-retaining strips	maple	$3/_{16}$	(5)	$1/_4$	(6)	$13^1/_4$+/-	(337)	45° miter both ends
N	4	glass-retaining strips	maple	$3/_{16}$	(5)	$1/_4$	(6)	6+/-	(152)	45° miter both ends
P	1	door stop	wenge	$1/_8$	(3)	$1/_4$	(6)	$16^1/_4$+/-	(413)	length +/-, fit strip between glass retaining strips Q
Q	4	glass-retaining strips	wenge	$1/_2$	(13)	$1/_2$	(13)	15	(381)	strips are triangular in cross section
R	2	brackets	plywood	$1/_2$	(13)	2+/-	(51)	10	(254)	bird's eye maple veneer plywood
S	2	gluing strips	wenge	$1/_2$	(13)	$1/_2$	(13)	$16^1/_2$	(419)	
T	2	gluing strips	wenge	$1/_2$	(13)	$1/_2$	(13)	10+/-	(254)	fit strips between the two long strips
U	2	door handles	padauk	$3/_8$	(10)	$3/_8$	(10)	$1^3/_4$	(45)	see illustration for details

HARDWARE

2   1" x $1^1/_2$" x $14^5/_8$" (25mm x 38mm x 371mm) continuous hinges

2   $1/_8$" x $5^3/_4$" x $13^1/_8$" (3mm x 146mm x 333mm) glass panels

2   $1/_8$" x $9^7/_8$" x $15^1/_{16}$" (3mm x 251mm x 383mm) glass panels

16   $1/_4$" x $3/_4$" (6mm x 19mm) gluing dowels

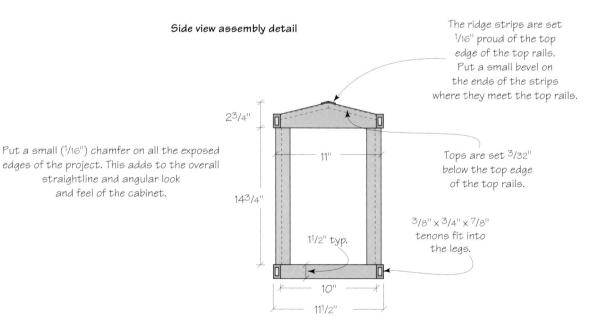

Side view assembly detail

The ridge strips are set $1/_{16}$" proud of the top edge of the top rails. Put a small bevel on the ends of the strips where they meet the top rails.

Put a small ($1/_{16}$") chamfer on all the exposed edges of the project. This adds to the overall straightline and angular look and feel of the cabinet.

Tops are set $3/_{32}$" below the top edge of the top rails.

$3/_8$" x $3/_4$" x $7/_8$" tenons fit into the legs.

$2^3/_4$"

$14^3/_4$"

11"

$1^1/_2$" typ.

10"

$11^1/_2$"

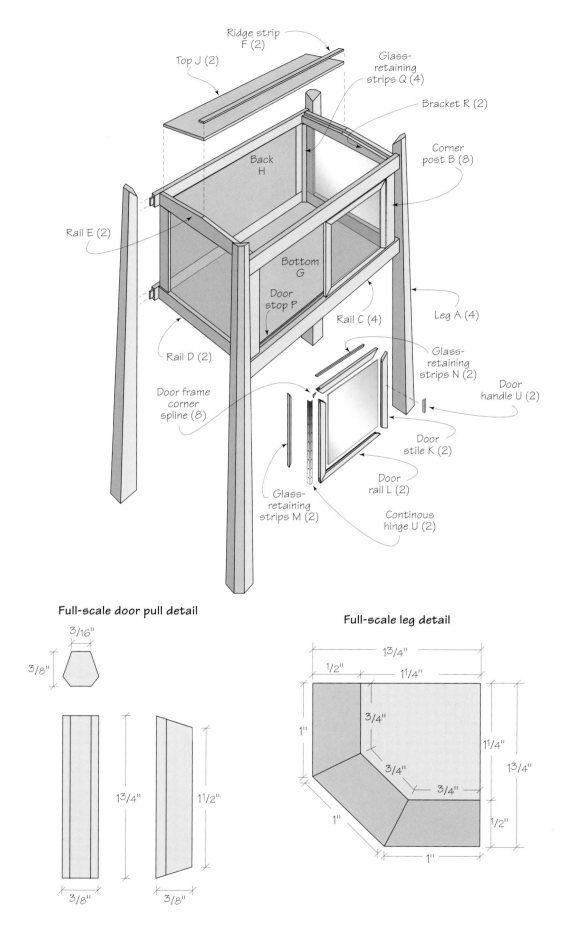

Ridge strip
F (2)

Top J (2)

Glass-
retaining
strips Q (4)

Bracket R (2)

Corner
post B (8)

Back
H

Rail E (2)

Leg A (4)

Bottom
G

Door
stop P

Rail C (4)

Rail D (2)

Glass-
retaining
strips N (2)

Door
handle U (2)

Door frame
corner
spline (8)

Door
stile K (2)

Glass-
retaining
strips M (2)

Door
rail L (2)

Continous
hinge U (2)

Full-scale door pull detail

3/16"

3/8"

13/4"

3/8"

11/2"

3/8"

Full-scale leg detail

13/4"

1/2"

11/4"

1"

3/4"

3/4"

11/4"

3/4"

13/4"

1"

1"

1/2"

tapering on the router table

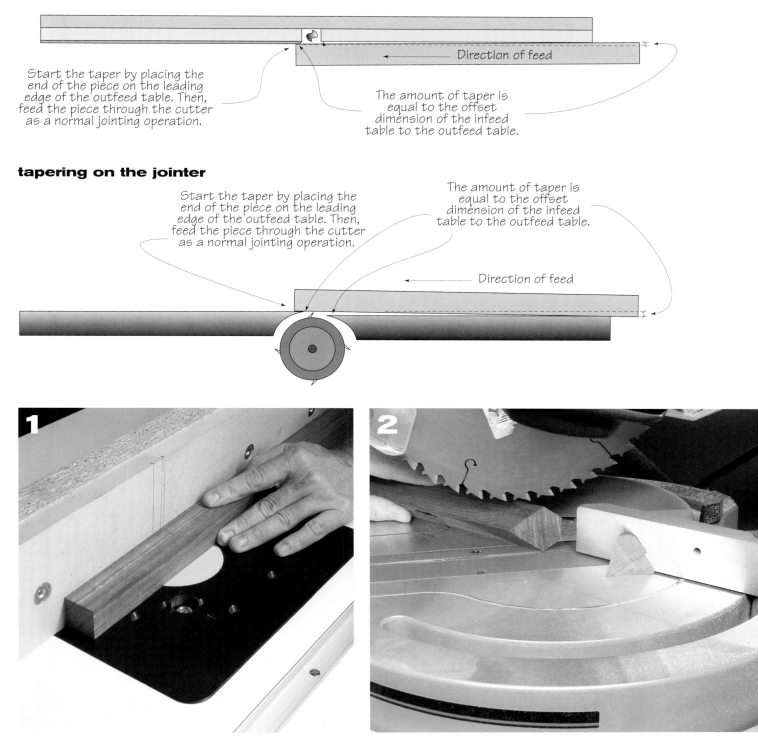

Start the taper by placing the end of the piece on the leading edge of the outfeed table. Then, feed the piece through the cutter as a normal jointing operation.

The amount of taper is equal to the offset dimension of the infeed table to the outfeed table.

Direction of feed

tapering on the jointer

Start the taper by placing the end of the piece on the leading edge of the outfeed table. Then, feed the piece through the cutter as a normal jointing operation.

The amount of taper is equal to the offset dimension of the infeed table to the outfeed table.

Direction of feed

1

Mark the locations of the mortises on the legs. Make marks on the router table fence showing the location of the router bit. This will give you the start and stop points for cutting the mortise. Hold the back part of the leg on the router tabletop and hold the rest of the leg over the router bit. Lower the leg onto the router bit, making a plunge cut. Then, feed the leg until the marks on the legs lineup with the marks on the router table fence. Lift up the front part of the leg off the router bit. Flip the leg end for end and cut the other mortises in the opposite side of the leg. All the legs need to be marked right and left front and right and left back to help you keep the legs in their proper locations.

2

Cut the 45° bevel at the tops of the legs. Hold the 45° flat taper on the front of the leg against the saw's vertical fence when making this cut. This bevel will taper to the inside of the cabinet diagonally at a 45° angle, adding visual movement to the entire project.

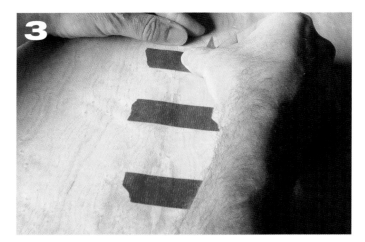

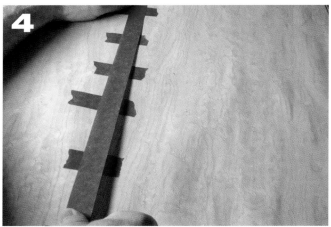

If you have some special wood you would like to use for the bottom, top and back panels, cut them as shown in the cutting list. If you are using veneer, start by jointing one edge of all the leaves of veneer. You can joint them all at one time by sandwiching them between two flat boards and running this setup on a jointer. You can also clamp the setup in a vise and plane the edges with a hand plane. Then, lay out the leaves in bookmatched patterns of your choice. Tape the butt-jointed edges of the veneer leaves together.

Run a piece of tape the length of the veneer joint. This will ensure the joint stays together during glue-up.

Use either a serrated trowel or a small paint roller to apply an even coat of glue to the substrate for the veneer. Do not apply any glue to the veneer or it will immediately start to curl and become difficult to place on the substrate.

Have all the clamps, clamping cauls and waxed paper ready to go when you start the veneer glue-up procedure. Put a sheet of waxed paper against each veneered surface to prevent the panels from sticking to the tabletop and to each other.

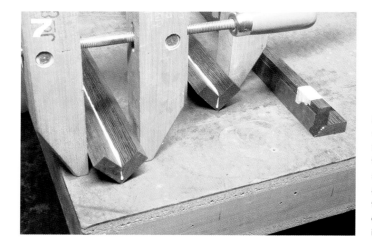

After cutting the 45° bevels on the corner posts, lay the parts faceup with the sharp edges of the miters touching. Tape this joint, turn the assembly over, apply glue to the joint and fold as shown in the photo. Hold the assembly together with light clamp pressure or wrap tape around it until the glue dries.

Using a straight-cutting bit set up in the router, cut the mortises in the front and back rails. Use the adjustable fences as limiting stops and a miter gauge as a guide to feed the work.

This method produces a clean mortise.

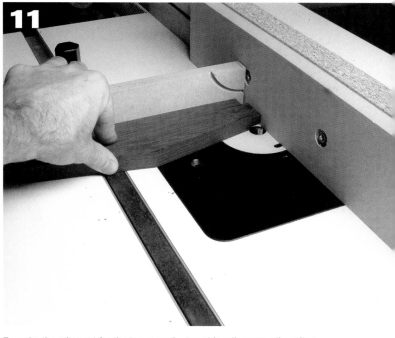

Set the straight-cutting bit to the proper height and cut the tenons on the side rails. Cut the tenon in two or three passes to nibble the material away. To cut the tenons on the top side rails, use the miter gauge on the straight side of the rail and make the cut.

To make the other cut for the tenon on the top side rail, reverse the miter gauge, flip the rail over and make the second cut.

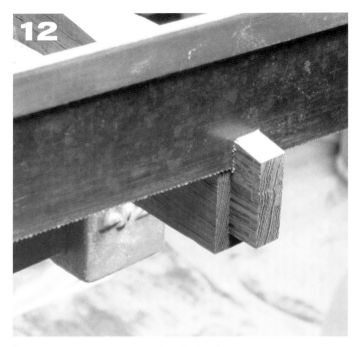

Cut the top shoulder on the top rails with a handsaw.

Make the second cut from the end of the tenon. Be careful not to cut into the shoulder.

Use a file to round the tenons.

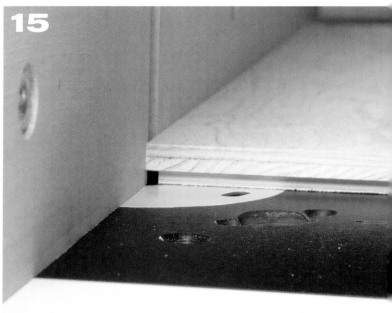

Cut the $1/8$" x $1/8$" rabbet on the bottom panel, using a straight-cutting bit.

16

doweling jig

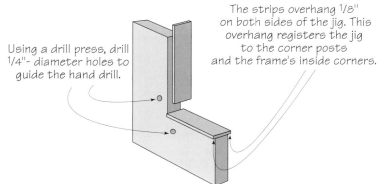

Using a drill press, drill 1/4"- diameter holes to guide the hand drill.

The strips overhang 1/8" on both sides of the jig. This overhang registers the jig to the corner posts and the frame's inside corners.

Set the bottom panel facedown on the work top and fit the bottom frame facedown around it. Use the beveled falloff strips left over from cutting the corner posts' bevels as glue blocks S and T. Glue them to the inside of the bottom. When the glue dries, the panel will be firmly in place. Then assemble the top frame.

17

Use dowels to locate and attach the corner posts to the top and bottom frame assemblies. Make a doweling jig as shown in the photo (see the illustration for details).

18

The lips of the attached strips will register the jig on the inside of the corner posts.

Use the doweling jig to drill holes in the top and bottom assemblies. The lip of the strips on the jig will register it on the inside corners of the frames. The lip will just fit into the rabbet in the bottom panel.

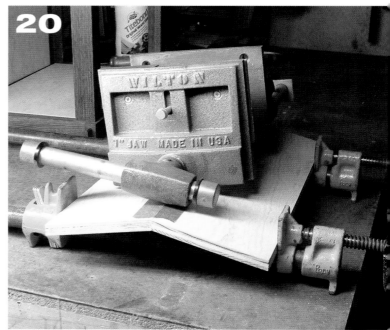

Cut the bevels on the top panels. Tape the miter joint, apply glue and fold it together. Lightly clamp the parts and counter the clamp pressure by putting some weight on the top of the joint.

Glue two corner posts to the sides of the back panel.

Cut two brackets to fit on the inside of the top frame and glue them in place. Use the top panel assembly to help locate these brackets. After the glue sets, remove the top panel, add glue to the top edges of the brackets and reinsert the top panel assembly, gluing it in place.

Dry fit all the parts before final assembly. Once you're sure it all fits together properly, add glue to the tenons and in the mortises. Using no more pressure than is needed, clamp the cabinet together. Double-check for squareness.

Glue the door stop into the front groove in the bottom of the cabinet.

Cut the miters on the top ridge strips. Tape the miters, glue and clamp them together. After the glue dries, cut the ridge strip assembly to length. Bevel the outside top edges of the assembly, then glue it to the top of the cabinet. Be sure the top ridge of the assembly lines up with the peaks of each top side rail.

After the glass is put into the cabinet, it is held in place with four triangular strips that are attached to the cabinet with $3/4$"- long brass screws.

28

Sand the legs. Attach the legs to the cabinet using glue.

29

The photo shows the beveled ends of the top rails where they join the front rails. The ridge strip assembly is also beveled on its long edges and at the ends where they meet the top side rails.

30

This photo shows the space between the leg and the side post and how the angles cut on the tops of the legs are oriented to the cabinet.

31

Machine the door frame parts to thickness and width. Leave the parts long. Cut the rabbets in the door frame parts using a rabbeting bit. This bit's cutter is ground to an angle that allows the cutter to shear the material. This makes a clean cut rabbet with no wood grain tear-out.

32

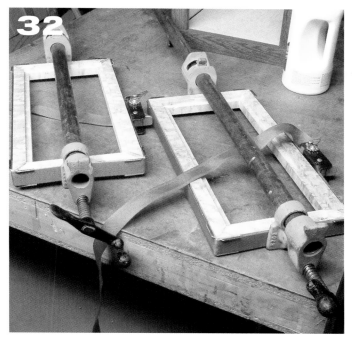

Measure the opening for the doors in the cabinet box. Cut the door parts accordingly. You want these doors to fit with a minimum amount of clearance on all sides. It gives the project a nice look. Using band clamps, glue the miter joints on each door. Don't use any fasteners in these joints. The glue will hold these doors together while you do the next machining operation.

33

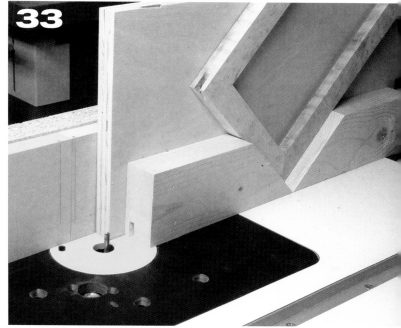

Using a slotting fixture, cut the slots in the corners of the door frames. Use a straight-cutting ¼"-diameter router bit.

Cut hardwood splines from the same material as the cabinet box frame is made of and glue them into the slots in the corners of the doors. These splines add the necessary strength to keep the miter joints strong and secure while adding another decorative element to the project. Attach the continuous hinges to the doors and install them in the cabinet. Attach the door handles. When everything fits properly, remove the doors and finish the entire cabinet and the doors. Install the glass in the doors and the cabinet. Then reinstall the doors.

34

shell boxes

I'M A TREE-HUGGING NATURE LOVER who also finds beauty in pure textbook geometry. The two areas of interest aren't mutually exclusive when you consider the mathematics inherent in a honeycomb, snowflake or the subject at hand — scallop shells. Scallop shells have been featured in art, architecture, religion and furniture design throughout history. When used as a furniture accent, the shell is usually the product of an expert carver.

The variable-incline-with-rotary-table jig that I developed for my shell box lids allows the average straight-line router user to produce something that closely approximates the geometrical beauty of the scallop with a single V-grooving bit. A quick Internet search on the subject of scallops will provide you with a glimpse into the infinite variety of shell patterns and colors. Almost any combination of woods will work. Because the jig requires a fair amount of labor in itself, plan on making a collection of shells. Once you have the jig, it's all (literally) downhill.

JOHN HUTCHINSON

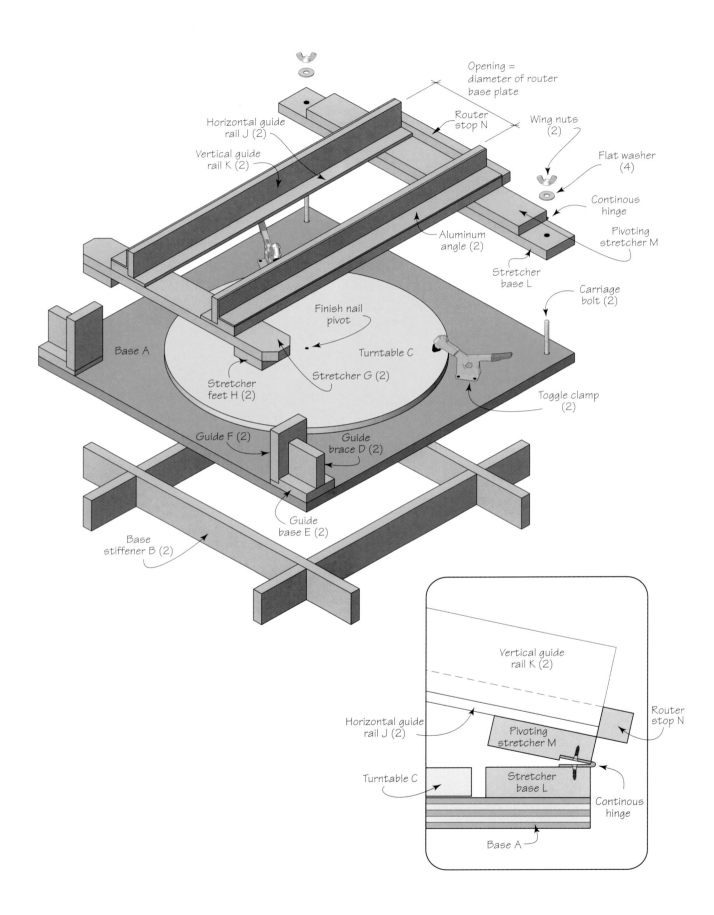

Opening = diameter of router base plate

Router stop N

Wing nuts (2)

Flat washer (4)

Horizontal guide rail J (2)

Vertical guide rail K (2)

Continous hinge

Pivoting stretcher M

Aluminum angle (2)

Stretcher base L

Carriage bolt (2)

Finish nail pivot

Base A

Turntable C

Stretcher feet H (2)

Stretcher G (2)

Toggle clamp (2)

Guide F (2)

Guide brace D (2)

Guide base E (2)

Base stiffener B (2)

Vertical guide rail K (2)

Router stop N

Horizontal guide rail J (2)

Pivoting stretcher M

Turntable C

Stretcher base L

Continous hinge

Base A

shell box router jig

inches (millimeters)

REFERENCE	QUANTITY	PART	STOCK	THICKNESS	(mm)	WIDTH	(mm)	LENGTH	(mm)	COMMENTS
A	1	base	plywood	3/4	(19)	24	(610)	24	(610)	
B	2	base stiffeners	plywood	3/4	(19)	2 1/2	(64)	24	(610)	half lap
C	1	turntable	plywood	1/2	(13)	18 dia.	(457)			
D	2	guide braces	poplar	3/4	(19)	2 1/2	(64)	2 1/2	(64)	
E	2	guide bases	poplar	3/4	(19)	2 1/2	(64)	3 1/4	(83)	3/4"-wide by 3/8"-deep (19mm by 10mm) rabbet one end
F	2	guides	poplar	3/4	(19)	2 1/2	(64)	4	(102)	
G	2	stretchers	poplar	3/4	(19)	2 1/2	(64)	17 1/2	(445)	3/4"-wide by 3/4"-deep (19mm by 19mm) rabbet both ends
H	2	stretcher feet	poplar	3/4	(19)	2 1/2	(64)	2 1/2	(64)	
J	2	horizontal guide rails	poplar	3/4	(19)	3	(76)	24	(610)	1 1/2"-wide by 1/2"-deep (38mm by 13mm) rabbet one edge
K	2	vertical guide rails	poplar	3/4	(19)	2	(51)	24	(610)	
L	1	stretcher base	poplar	3/4	(19)	2 1/2	(64)	24	(610)	
M	1	pivoting stretcher	poplar	3/4	(19)	2 1/2	(64)	19	(483)	
N	1	router stop	poplar	3/4	(19)	3/4	(19)			length = the router base plate diameter + 1 1/2" (38mm)

HARDWARE

1	16d finish nail
2	toggle clamps
2	1 1/2" x 1 1/2" x 24" (38mm x 38mm x 610mm) aluminum angle
2	3/8"-16 x 3" (80mm) carriage bolts
2	3/8"-16 (10mm) wing nuts
4	3/8" (10mm) flat washers
1	3/4" x 1 1/2" x 19" (19mm x 38mm x 483mm) continuous hinge

shell box

inches (millimeters)

REFERENCE	QUANTITY	PART	STOCK	THICKNESS	(mm)	WIDTH	(mm)	LENGTH	(mm)	COMMENTS
A	3	lid segments	mahogany	3/4	(19)	4	(102)	7 1/4	(184)	
B	1	tail	red oak	3/8	(10)	1 3/8	(35)	3 1/8	(79)	
C	1	box	red oak	1 3/8	(35)	6 3/4	(171)	7 13/16	(198)	if making deeper box, build up to desired thickness
D	1	bottom	baltic birch	1/8	(3)	6 3/4	(171)	7 13/16	(198)	plywood

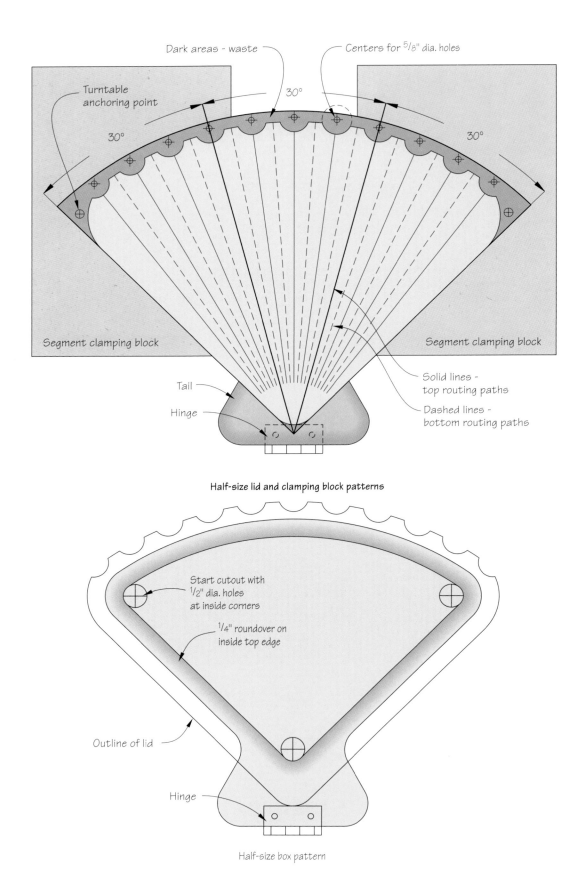

Dark areas - waste

Centers for $5/8$" dia. holes

Turntable
anchoring point

30°

30°

30°

30°

Segment clamping block

Segment clamping block

Tail

Hinge

Solid lines -
top routing paths

Dashed lines -
bottom routing paths

Half-size lid and clamping block patterns

Start cutout with
$1/2$" dia. holes
at inside corners

$1/4$" roundover on
inside top edge

Outline of lid

Hinge

Half-size box pattern

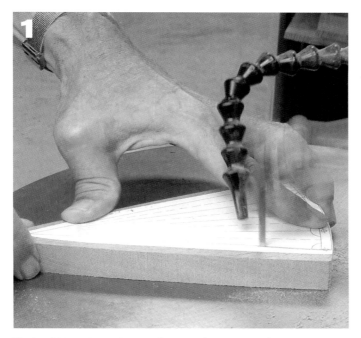

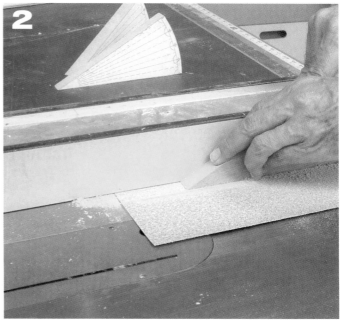

The box lid is made up of three 30° triangles (see illustration). Following an application of spray adhesive, apply one of the segment patterns to ¾" stock with the center line of the pattern parallel to the long grain. The ribs of a seashell radiate out from a center point. The three-part segmentation of the lid mimics Mother Nature. Rather than worrying over angles on a miter gauge, I simply cut the parts out with a scroll saw, staying slightly wide of the pattern lines.

I like to stay away from the table saw when cutting small parts, but it does come in handy from time to time as an edge jointer. After locking a piece of sandpaper under the fence, a few firm passes of each triangle over the paper, with one face tight to the fence, assures me of some airtight joints.

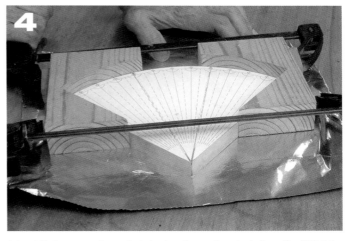

A couple of clamping blocks, a liberal application of glue and some aluminum foil borrowed from the kitchen are all I need to start getting it all together.

A few 12" clamps are the perfect size for glue-up. In order to keep the lid flat, I like to keep them low on the assembly and as parallel to the table as possible. The aluminum foil prevents the lid from becoming a permanent table decoration.

After allowing the glue to cure, and removing the squeeze-out, I turn to the drill press and, with a $\frac{5}{8}$" Forstner bit, drill the 11 holes on the leading edge of the shell.

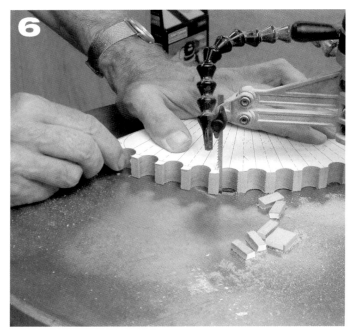

Back on the scroll saw, I remove the little nubs left between the holes.

Rather than experimenting on my precious segmented shell stock, I screw an extra segment, with an adhesive-applied pattern, to the shell box router jig's turntable. I'm careful to make sure that the point of the triangle is directly over the center of the pivot nail.

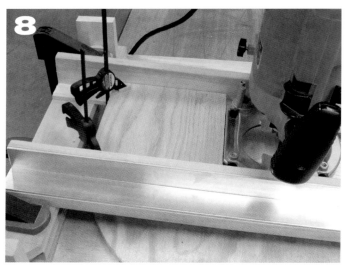

By shimming the back stretcher on the jig, I set the angle on the guide rails. A stop (or maybe that should be "start") block clamped between the rails defines the starting point for every cut. The larger clamps hold the shims in place and secure the jig to the workbench.

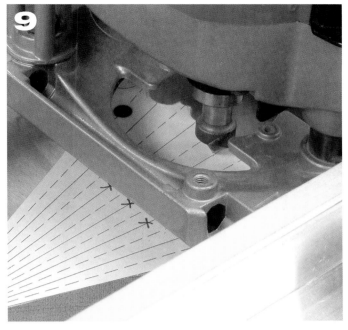

With the motor off, and the 90° V-grooving bit locked in a partial plunge position, I swing the turntable until the center of my cutting path aligns with the center of the bit. When I'm satisfied with its position, I engage the toggle clamps, raise the bit, and return the router to its starting position.

And now the fun begins. At the starting line, I bring the router up to speed, plunge, lock and push. Smooth, gentle pressure produces the best cuts. Let the bit do the cutting; we're not plowing here.

Once I'm satisfied with the angle of the cut, and I've gotten into the rhythm of forming the ribs, I screw the segmented shell stock to the table and complete the top cuts.

With the top cut, I turn the lid over, apply a fresh segment pattern, screw it to the table, and follow the same cutting steps, this time following the bottom routing paths.

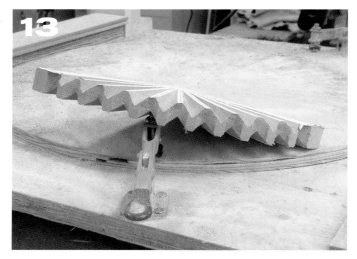

Success! What started as a few triangles of wood is now taking on some aquatic life.

With the labor of 21 radial plunge cuts behind me, I return to the scroll saw and remove the waste at the three corners of the lid. Again, stay slightly wide of the line and smooth the corners on a spindle sander.

With a ¼"-radius roundover bit installed in the router table, I round the top two continuous edges of the lid only. Stay away from the scalloped edge. The sharp sawtooth character of the leading edge is a great contrast to the softness of the sides.

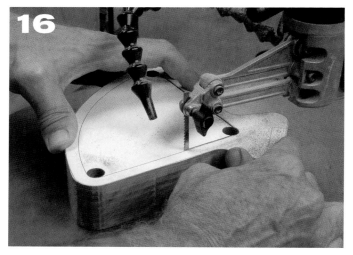

I start the box portion of the project by drilling ½"-diameter holes at the three corners of the thick box stock. After that, it's back to the scroll saw for the inside and outside cuts.

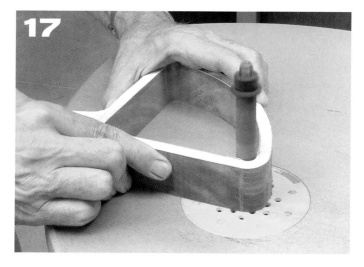

The spindle sander makes quick work of inside and outside sanding chores.

Back at the router table, I use the ¼"-radius roundover bit to soften the top inside edge of the box.

For the box bottom, I decided to go with the simplicity of ⅛" Baltic birch plywood. I wasn't happy with the industrial look of the plywood relative to the organic look of the box and lid, so I undercut it with a miniature 45° chamfering bit.

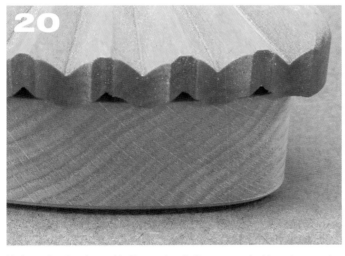

Undercutting the plywood bottom makes it disappear and adds a nice reveal shadow line at the base.

After a little cutting, fitting and rounding, I glue the ⅛"-thick tail to the shell.

At almost $20 per pair, the solid-brass, 95° stopped hinges that I selected for the box may seem like an extravagance. They are, however, the heart of the bivalve. Once you've installed them, they'll seem like a bargain. Besides, the extra hinge is a natural excuse for the next box. Try a layered box next for some additional storage room.

suppliers

ADAMS & KENNEDY – THE WOOD SOURCE
6178 Mitch Owen Road
P.O. Box 700
Manotick, Ontario, Canada K4M 1A6
613-822-6800
www.wood-source.com
Wood supply

B&Q
B&Q Head Office
Portswood House
1 Hampshire Corporate Park
Chandlers Ford
Eastleigh
Hants
SO53 3YX
0870 0101 006
www.diy.com
Tools, paint, wood, electrical, garden

BRIMARC ASSOCIATES
7-9 Ladbroke Park
Millers Road
Warwick
CV34 5AE
01926 493389
www.brimarc.com
Woodworking tools and accessories

THE CANING SHOP
926 Gilman Street
Berkeley, California 94710
800-544-3373
www.caning.com
Shaker tape and caning supplies

CONNECTICUT CANE AND REED COMPANY
P.O. Box 762
Manchester, Connecticut 06045
800-227-8498
www.caneandreed.com
Cane and reed materials

CONSTANTINES WOOD CENTER OF FLORIDA, INC.
1040 East Oakland Park Boulevard
Fort Lauderdale, Florida 33334
800-443-9667
www.constantines.com
Tools, woods, veneers, hardware

FOCUS (DIY) LIMITED
Gawsworth House
Westmere Drive
Crewe
Cheshire
CW1 6XB
0800 436 436
www.focusdiy.co.uk
Tools and home woodworking equipment

HOUSE OF TOOLS
100 Mayfield Common Northwest
Edmonton, Alberta, Canada T5P 4B3
800-661-3987
www.houseoftools.com
Woodworking tools and hardware

HOMEBASE LTD
Beddington House
Railway Approach
Wallington
Surrey
SM6 OHB
0845 077 8888
www.homebase.co.uk
Tools and home woodworking equipment

THE HOME DEPOT
2455 Paces Ferry Road
Atlanta, Georgia 30339
800-553-3199 (U.S.)
800-668-2266 (Canada)
www.homedepot.com
Tools, paint, wood, electrical, garden

LANGEVIN & FOREST
9995 Boulevard Pie IX
Montreal, Quebec, Canada H1Z 3X1
800-889-2060
www.langevinforest.com
Tools, wood and books

LEE VALLEY TOOLS LTD. & VERITAS TOOLS INC.
U.S.:
P.O. Box 1780
Ogdensburg, New York 13669-6780
800-267-8735
Canada:
P.O. Box 6295, Station J
Ottawa, Ontario, Canada K2A 1T4
800-267-8761
www.leevalley.com
Bench dogs and other bench hardware